ENHANCE YOUR DESTINY

DARE TO BUILD A SECOND LIFE

Elwood N. Chapman

CRISP PUBLICATIONS, INC.
Los Altos, California

ENHANCE YOUR DESTINY
DARE TO BUILD A SECOND LIFE

Elwood N. Chapman

CREDITS
Editor: **Michael Crisp**
Layout and Composition: **Interface Studio**
Cover Design: **Carol Harris**
Artwork: **Ralph Mapson**

Copyright © 1992 by Crisp Publications, Inc.
Printed in the United States of America

English language Crisp books are distributed worldwide. Our major international distributors include:

CANADA: Reid Publishing, LTD., Box 7267, Oakville, Ontario Canada L6J 6L6. TEL: (416) 842-4428, FAX: (416) 842-9327

AUSTRALIA: Career Builders, P. O. Box 1051, Springwood, Brisbane, Queensland, Australia 4127. TEL: 841-1061, FAX: 841-1580

NEW ZEALAND: Career Builders, P. O. Box 571, Manurewa, Auckland, New Zealand. TEL: 266-5276, FAX: 266-4152

JAPAN: Phoenix Associates Co., Mizuho Bldg. 2-12-2, Kami Osaki, Shinagawa-Ku, Tokyo 141, Japan. TEL: 3-443-7231, FAX: 3-443-7640

Selected Crisp titles are also available in other languages. Contact International Rights Manager Tim Polk at (415) 949-4888 for more information.

Library of Congress Catalog Card Number 90-85865
Chapman, Elwood N.
Enhance Your Destiny
ISBN 1-56052-100-7

PREFACE

Upon my retirement at age 61, I wrote *Comfort Zones: Planning Your Future*. Thanks to sales of more than 100,000 copies, I revised it and added a video three years later. Several readers of *Comfort Zones* urged me to produce a book that encouraged people to start their retirement planning earlier. Initial progress on this challenge was slow—but then I asked myself: "What would I do if I were 40?"

Then it hit me!

People should do early retirement planning because it has the potential to enhance their present lives. Whether individuals have a successful retirement is secondary. *It is what happens to the quality of their present lives that is important.*

You may not, at this point, accept the "two lives philosophy" as big news. Whatever your views, please consider the following:

- A retirement revolution is taking place. Old stereotypes and misconceptions are disappearing. "Retirement" in today's world places increased emphasis on more years, better health, and the potential for a rewarding "second life."

- Because of tough economic times, workers are more negative about their careers today. A few say openly that the only thing they have to look forward to is *not working*. These people need to learn that the process of planning an exciting retirement can turn their negative attitudes about their present career around.

- Early planning (when done with enthusiasm) can enhance expectations, release creative talents, and give all aspects of one's present life new meaning.

Early retirement planning pays off twice—now and later!

Good luck!

Elwood N. Chapman

i

ACKNOWLEDGEMENTS

It has been my practice to interview people about their attitudes toward retirement. Most of the vignettes and concepts in this book have been developed from these interviews. The people I interviewed fall into three categories:

1. Professionals who use my retirement planning book *Comfort Zones* in their seminars.

2. People who attended my lectures aboard the Crown Odyssey of the Royal Cruise Lines.

3. And those who reside in our small town of Seal Beach, California.

The interviews were supplemented by research from professional journals and other publications in the field of gerontology.

Although no attempt was made to keep a list of those interviewed, I do thank them for being generous with their time and insights. A very special thanks is acknowledged to those who made a significant contribution to the manuscript, including:

> Louise Berman—Retirement Planner
> Pam Conway—Training Director, Discovery Card Services
> Mike Crisp—Publisher
> Pat Heim, Ph.D.—Professional Trainer
> Mary Jo Henricksen—Retired School Teacher
> William Kaufman—Publisher
> Robert Maddux—Vice President, Right Associates
> Jack and Marise Sisson—Dance Instructors
> C. Paxton Stodder, M.D.—Physician

I would be negligent if I did not mention the major contribution of my wife, Martha. Not only does she edit my material, but she critiques my thoughts before I can get them on paper. Most importantly, she protects me from the interruptions of the outside world on my writing days.

E.N. Chapman

DEDICATION

THREE BOOKS IN ONE

In reality, this is three books under one cover. The first asks you to look at your future, the second helps you plan for it, and the third dares you to predict what your second life could be like. The first book is traditional. It is read like any other title. The second is a planning guide that should be read with a pencil in hand. Consider it to be a personalized ''workbook'' that will help you complete a realistic plan for a more fulfilling second life. Book III provides a picture of what your second life may be like by dividing it into five different zones, each of which contributes to a positive ''second life.''

As you read Book I, keep in mind that it was designed to show you the potential your life has and to help you turn your life (from this day forward) into a positive adventure.

Once you have completed *Enhance Your Destiny* you will have, perhaps for the first time, an optimistic, realistic plan for a meaningful future.

CONTENTS

**BOOK I   IMAGINE! TWO FULL LIVES
            FOR THE PRICE OF ONE**

BOOK II   SECOND LIFE PLANNING GUIDE

CONTENTS (Continued)

BOOK I

IMAGINE! TWO FULL LIVES FOR THE PRICE OF ONE

DESTINY

"A real or imaginary power or agency conceived as pre-determining the course of events and choice of alternatives."

Webster's Third New International Dictionary. Unabridged. (3)

Chapter 1
DEVELOP A BRAVE, NEW
TWO-LIFE PHILOSOPHY

> *"It's not later than you think, it's sooner than you suspect."*
>
> Anonymous

For the first time in history, we have the opportunity to live *two* successful and fulfilling lives while we are on this earth. My experience has shown that too often, people close their minds to the possibility and view their second life (retirement) as little more than a release from the frustrations of work. These individuals unnecessarily downgrade both lives. The solution is to develop a "two-life" attitude.

FORGET THE R WORD

To assist you in developing a two-life attitude, the words "second life" will be substituted. This is because:

- A second life means a new beginning. The word retirement suggests backing away from life and its challenges.

- There are too many myths, stereotypes, and negative connotations connected with the word retirement. *Using the R word perpetuates erroneous thinking.*

- The term "second life" is more accurate because it communicates that a revolution is taking place. *This revolution is giving individuals more years, better health, earlier release from full-time work, and greater opportunities for fulfillment.*

If thinking about two lives seems awkward, please be patient. We are talking about a new attitude that is difficult to develop quickly. Once you become comfortable with this new way of thinking (and resist using the R word), a door will open and you will view your present life in a more expansive and exciting manner.

At this point, it is natural to have questions. Do most people have enough money, energy, and desire for a *true* second life? Is there enough time and variety of experiences for two full lives? Can people really enhance their destinies by creating a second life for themselves? These, and similar questions, will be answered in this book.

FIGURING YOUR LIFE EXPECTANCY

To start, please read the statistics in the box that follows, then figure your life expectancy from the table on the facing page. As you do this, keep in mind that the trend is for expectancy tables to constantly be revised upward.

SOME SECOND-LIFE STATISTICS

- In 1900 life expectancy was 47. Today it is 75.

- Rand Corporation projects that, because of improved health care, disease prevention, genetic engineering, and other advances, life expectancy at birth may reach 90 shortly after the turn of the century.

- More and more people are living to be 100.

- Marriages of 65, 75, and 80 years are becoming more common.

- Since 1969, the over-65 group has grown more than twice as fast as the rest of the population.

Using the statistics, my life expectancy is ____ years. Subtracting my current age means I should have approximately ____ years to develop "two lives for the price of one."

VITAL STATISTICS

AGE IN 1986 (years)	EXPECTATION OF LIFE IN YEARS				
	Total	White		Black	
		Male	Female	Male	Female
20	56.2	53.4	59.9	47.3	55.3
21	55.2	52.5	58.9	46.4	54.3
22	54.3	51.5	57.9	45.5	53.3
23	53.3	50.6	56.9	44.6	52.4
24	52.4	49.7	56.0	43.7	51.4
25	51.5	48.8	55.0	42.8	50.5
26	50.5	47.9	54.0	42.0	49.5
27	49.6	47.0	53.1	41.1	48.6
28	48.7	46.0	52.1	40.2	47.6
29	47.7	45.1	51.1	39.4	46.7
30	46.8	44.2	50.1	38.5	45.7
31	45.8	43.2	49.2	37.7	44.8
32	44.9	42.3	48.2	36.8	43.9
33	44.0	41.4	47.2	36.0	43.0
34	43.0	40.5	46.3	35.2	42.1
35	42.1	39.5	45.3	34.3	41.1
36	41.2	38.6	44.3	33.5	40.2
37	40.2	37.7	43.4	32.7	39.3
38	39.3	36.8	42.4	31.9	38.4
39	38.4	35.9	41.5	31.1	37.5
40	37.4	34.9	40.5	30.3	36.6
41	36.5	34.0	39.6	29.5	35.7
42	35.6	33.1	38.6	28.7	34.8
43	34.7	32.2	37.7	28.0	34.0
44	33.8	31.3	36.7	27.2	33.1
45	32.9	30.4	35.8	26.4	32.2
46	32.0	29.5	34.9	25.7	31.4
47	31.1	28.7	33.9	24.9	30.5
48	30.2	27.8	33.0	24.1	29.7
49	29.4	26.9	32.1	23.4	28.8
50	28.5	26.1	31.2	22.7	28.0
51	27.6	25.2	30.3	22.0	27.2
52	26.8	24.4	29.4	21.3	26.4
53	26.0	23.6	28.6	20.6	25.6
54	25.1	22.7	27.7	19.9	24.8
55	24.3	21.9	26.8	19.3	24.0
56	23.5	21.2	26.0	18.6	23.3
57	22.7	20.4	25.1	18.0	22.5
58	21.9	19.6	24.3	17.3	21.8
59	21.2	18.9	23.4	16.7	21.0
60	20.4	18.2	22.6	16.1	20.3
61	19.7	17.5	21.8	15.5	19.6
62	18.9	16.8	21.0	15.0	19.0
63	18.2	16.1	20.2	14.4	18.3
64	17.5	15.4	19.5	13.9	17.7
65	16.8	14.8	18.7	13.4	17.0
70	13.6	11.7	15.1	10.8	13.9
75	10.7	9.1	11.8	8.7	11.1
80	8.1	6.9	8.8	6.8	8.5
85 and over	6.0	5.1	6.4	5.5	6.7

Source: U.S. National Center for Health Statistics, *Vital Statistics of the United States*, annual.

ANSWER THESE QUESTIONS

Noting your life expectancy number, answer these questions:

	Yes	No	Undecided
1. Do you think that a "two-life philosophy" will improve your future?	☐	☐	☐
2. If you spent years of formal and on-the-job education preparing for your first life, shouldn't you be willing to devote some time preparing for your second?	☐	☐	☐

To help you gain a two-life attitude, consider these comments from an alert centenarian:

> *"I will be 100 years old next Valentine's day. I worked hard at various jobs until I was 60. Then I started a new life that now seems longer and more bountiful than the first. Although I have done well, with more planning in my early years I could have done far better. Tell your young readers not to underestimate the magnificent opportunities that exist after retirement."*

YOU PAY THE PRICE WHETHER YOU COLLECT OR NOT

Much of what we do in our first life is preparation for a second life, even though we may not get excited about it. For example, many of us work hard, save money, and delay gratifications. We pay a stiff price. How stiff? Perhaps the following questions will tell:

- How much is deducted monthly from your earnings for Social Security benefits?
- Are you contributing to a retirement plan annuity, or insurance program that you can cash in later?
- Is job stress taking place that is caused by long commutes, organizational changes, keeping up with technology or human relations conflicts?
- Are you a member of the "sandwich generation" caught between taking care of your immediate family (children) on one side, and parents or grandparents on the other?

If your answers to these questions are typical, you will probably agree that people pay a high price indeed. As high as the price has become, for many it is much higher than necessary. For example, some people permit themselves to get so discouraged with their first lives that they give up on the idea of a rewarding second life long before they get there. Through their attitudes, many wish simply to get *through* their "first life." What happens afterwards does not concern them. These unfortunate people pay the price and then walk away from the benefits!

ISN'T IT TIME TO JAZZ UP YOUR FIRST LIFE BY ANTICIPATING YOUR SECOND?

A new attitude is needed to get yourself on a "two-life" track. It is essential to *perceive* and anticipate two successful lives before you can make the most of either.

Only when you become excited and rejuvenated by the promise of second-life rewards will you start to enhance your destiny and become more enthusiastic about your present situation.

Chapter 2
THE TRIVIA TRAP MAY GET YOU LATER IF YOU DON'T PLAN NOW

> *"The mass of men lead lives of quiet desperation."*
> Henry David Thoreau

There is a major roadblock to a fulfilling second life—a problem so pervasive it is difficult to avoid. Gerontologists call it trivialization. As suggested in Chapter 1, many individuals work long hours and deny themselves pleasure in their first lives. These same people wind up feeling empty in their second lives because they do not have important goals.

The result?

Trivia takes over. People fill precious hours with busywork, or even worse, meaningless activities such as excessive television. Many individuals create unnecessary chores because such activities shorten their days. It doesn't seem to matter whether these chores provide pleasure or fulfillment. All that is required is that the activity uses up some time.

What is the basic cause for trivialization? Were the first lives so busy with undesirable work that idleness is rewarding? Is some of it due to inadequate education? Is there an inability to plan? A few answers are listed below.

THE DYNAMIC MINORITY

Wanting more information about trivialization, I decided to seek some answers. To motivate myself I set a goal of finding ten individuals who had avoided trivialization in their second lives. From these interviews I hoped to gain some insights. It took almost fifty interviews to find ten people who, in my opinion, had goals powerful enough to keep them away from too much busywork. All ten who avoided trivialization had the following serious involvements.

1. *An intense interest in photography.* This man attended many classes on photography, set up his own complete darkroom, entered contests and even sold a few of his best photographic efforts.

2. *An environmental activist.* This woman has made it her personal mission to protect wetlands from a proposed housing development. She won the battle and now conducts tours of the wetlands involved. She has developed a considerable knowledge of shorebirds.

3. *A grandchild day care center.* This woman is fulfilled by taking care of five small children so her daughters can work full-time.

4. *Church activities.* This interviewee is proud of her church role. She is chairperson of the endowment committee and devotes more than 20 hours each week to her church.

5. *Crops of fruit and flowers.* This woman gained her identity from having the most beautiful flower garden in the community. She routinely distributes fruit and flowers to family and friends.

6. *A musical group.* This engineer, upon retirement, turned his hobby of playing the saxaphone into a part-time career. He plays with a small group at community dances and special events.

7. *Dancing.* This couple followed their passion for dancing to the point that they started to give lessons. They are now in the process of opening their own studio.

8. *Fundraising.* Now president of a non-profit animal shelter, this woman is deeply involved in fund-raising. She raised over $50,000 to build the shelter on city-donated property.

9. *Traveling in a RV.* This man spent almost 300 days last year traveling to different parts of the United States. His mission is to help those who have problems on the road.

10. *Building and selling mountain cabins.* This couple is involved in building inexpensive mountain retreats for others. Most jobs are contracted out to meet the specifications of buyers.

LATE-BLOOMING GOALS

Second-life goals or purposes are not common and are highly individualistic. Those listed on page 11 generated interest, motivation, and involvement for the person interviewed. Had I interviewed another hundred individuals, a range of new interests would have been found.

What about the majority interviewed who were unable to articulate a goal? Did they all fall into the trivia trap? The answer is no. A number found that pleasure lifestyles kept them motivated and away from excessive busy work. These individuals often belonged to a variety of social groups (country clubs, senior centers, etc.) where participation in activities was almost a daily event.

Based on my informal interviews, most second-lifers seem to fall into one of three categories.

1. *Fulfillment Seekers:* These fortunate individuals have developed a purpose that keeps them motivated. Sometimes their involvement augments their incomes. More often they are volunteers. People in this group are *seeking something beyond pure pleasure.* They want to contribute to some cause or artistic endeavor that has significance to them.

2. *Pleasure Seekers:* Through a blend of travel, sports activities, social involvements, and other planned activities, these people make enjoyable use of free time. They are not interested in more serious goals, but they are able to minimize trivialization. Pleasure seekers rightfully take pride in the lifestyles they have created for themselves. Most have comfortable incomes.

3. *Time Fillers:* The majority who fall into this category are individuals without a plan. Their lives consist of trivial pursuits. Most rely heavily on television and seem to have little interest in searching for personal fulfillment or getting involved socially.

As might be expected, Fulfillment Seekers like to discuss the two-life idea because they are already making their lives more meaningful. Pleasure Seekers often back away from the concept because they fear becoming too involved in a cause. Time Fillers, whether because of income, age, health, or attitude, find it almost impossible to view retirement as a second life with countless opportunities.

DARING TO LOOK AHEAD

What is worth remembering from the interviews? The following factors may be significant:

- Without enthusiastic searching and planning, trivialization is predictable.
- Finding a purpose for one's second life can be as important and difficult as finding the best career for one's first life.
- Well-planned pleasure lifestyles decrease the possibility of trivialization, but appear less fulfilling than having a more defined purpose.

FINALLY DOING YOUR OWN THING

As is true of one's first life, a second life takes on a pattern of its own. No two lifestyles are the same. Some people make a conscious decision to take certain parts of their first life into their second. For example, they may take their work or profession with them on a part-time basis. Others elect to stay in homes and keep their community involvements.

Some people *need* to take first life involvements with them because they do not have anything else planned. Their second life becomes, to some extent, an extension of their first. Others do it by preference. These people consciously decide that they want a second life much the same as their first, but without all the pressures and responsibilities.

A few seek a fresh start. They perceive their second life as a new adventure and proceed to discard what occupied them in their first lives. These individuals feel the need to start from scratch. They seek something beyond work, money, power, or status. Instead of using their second lives to drain out every drop of satisfaction from first life goals, they seek new goals with new rewards. Rather than hanging onto the past, they set out to satisfy themselves. Rather than blur the line of demarcation between their two lives, they make a major effort to separate them.

These are the people who have the greatest success to enhance their destiny. Later in this book, you will learn how to join this dynamic minority.

Chapter 3
WINNING BIG AT BOTH ENDS

> *"When a man does not know what harbor he is making for, no wind is the right wind."*
> Seneca (4 B.C.–A.D. 65)

The way to win in "both lives" is to make self-motivating promises early in your first life and convert them into reality in your second. The "first life" promises become the goals you need for success in your "second life."

What constitutes a self-motivating goal? Three rules generally apply.

Rule 1 The promise or goal you make to yourself must come from a deep-seated desire within you. It cannot be manufactured.

Rule 2 The promise must fit within your personal comfort zone. It must be in harmony with your style, your needs, your personality. It must be important to *you*. How others view your choice is not important.

Rule 3 The promise must be realistic and reachable.

How does a person come up with such goals or promises? There is one simple requirement. *The goal must be one of significance that circumstances in your first life have prevented you from reaching.* A good way to discover such a challenge is to ask yourself: "What would I do with my life if I were totally free?"

THERE'S A BETTER LIFESTYLE WAITING

A few years ago I devised an exercise called *IRA: Inventory of Retirement Activities.** By answering a series of 54 statements, it is possible for a person to establish the degree of interest she or he has in eighteen categories shown on the next page.

---

* Crisp Publications, Inc., 95 First Street, Los Altos, Ca. 94022. Copyright E. N. Chapman.

```
┌─────────────────────────────────────────────────────────────┐
│              EIGHTEEN RETIREMENT ACTIVITIES                  │
│   ☐ Travel           ☐ Sports          ☐ Religious Activities│
│   ☐ Hobbies          ☐ Hobbies         ☐ Outdoor Activities  │
│      (Mechanical)       (Artistic)      ☐ Home Activities     │
│   ☐ Time Alone       ☐ Games           ☐ Social Activities    │
│   ☐ Television       ☐ Reading         ☐ Working Part Time    │
│   ☐ Investments      ☐ Family          ☐ Private Discussions  │
│   ☐ Volunteering     ☐ Education                             │
└─────────────────────────────────────────────────────────────┘
```

The purpose of the IRA exercise is to get people *thinking* about activities available to them. Once completed, a person has a clear idea of how they value spending time. When this is known, some specific goals can be prepared to allow for meaningful activities.

Once tentative goals have been selected, a second-life blueprint or roadmap can be prepared. Ideally, the blueprint should be started as early as possible in life, and expanded and refined until entry into a second life. This period of change and revision (perhaps lasting twenty years) should be considered as the "preparation" stage.

How do you know if you are on the right track? Stated simply, if the blueprint does not excite you and make your first life better, it is a weak plan and is not fulfilling its purpose.

WHY PEOPLE PROCRASTINATE

What are the hurdles that keep people from designing a second life blueprint years in advance? Here are three.

1. *"Retirement is too far into the future."* When you are thirty or forty it is difficult to imagine not having your career or family obligations. Many people come to the conclusion that they are better off thinking about today, instead of planning for a future that may never arrive.

2. *"I'd rather play it by ear."* In the past, almost everyone was satisfied to save some money and trust to luck when their second-life period arrived. These individuals tend to figure that changes made now will become obsolete in the future.

WHY PEOPLE PROCRASTINATE (Continued)

3. *"I'm too busy coping with my present life."* Living is a more complex matter that it used to be. There are more problems to face. Stresses are greater. Trying to do a plan now would only add more stress.

These barriers need to be respected, but they all ignore one significant factor. A little planning can not only prepare one for a quality second life but it can also enhance day-to-day living now.

THE SOONER YOU START THE SOONER YOU BENEFIT.

Each individual must determine just what she or he wishes to do with a second life. It is similar to the process you went through discovering your career goal. It requires exploration, thinking, and decision-making. *But it can be accomplished one step at a time as you live and improve your first life.*

The two projects go hand in hand. One compliments the other.

WHAT CONSTITUTES A SECOND-LIFE BLUEPRINT?

A second life blueprint is a tentative roadmap that is never completed. One starts out with a preliminary idea and continues to improve and refine it until the time arrives to put it into operation. Just as one starts searching for a career in high school or college, one should start designing a plan for a second life ten or more years ahead of time. Just as one needs a diploma of some sort to enter adult life, one needs a blueprint to enter a second life.

To provide you with an idea of what a preliminary blueprint might be for three individuals or couples, the facing page provides some abbrieviated models. These are starting points only. All need to be financed, augmented, and refined. If possible, activities should be started in advance of retirement on a part-time basis.

THREE SAMPLE BLUEPRINTS

PRELIMINARY MODEL A

Live in a small home or condo where less upkeep is required. Take at least one major trip to a new location each year. Engage in some form of creative effort—painting, writing, woodworking. When at home, contribute some time each week at a volunteer group. Play more bridge and get better at it. Spend more time in my garden. Etc.

PRELIMINARY MODEL B

Live in a cabin on a lake where I can watch the seasons come and go, enjoy a boat, and explore trails with my grandchildren. Learn to do better at competitive sports, especially golf, poker, and word games. Spend more time developing a new spiritualism. Do more reading. Spend time improving my home. Etc.

PRELIMINARY MODEL C

Work with my spouse restoring antique automobiles. Use the money we make to travel to antique car rallies. Build some new relationships. Stay as independent as possible. Get into home video production for family tapes. Maintain a daily health pattern where both of us participate. Etc.

TIPS ON HOW TO GET STARTED

Professional financial planners always ask their clients to provide them with a second-life goal so a financial strategy can be devised to help them reach that goal. Easy to say. Hard to do.

Following are some tips on how to start your blueprint:

- Start a second-life file so you will have tangible evidence you are on your way. Keep it with your other important papers. Discuss new ideas with your spouse or friends.

- Investigate what people you admire are doing with *their* lives. Be curious. Ask questions. If you find someone living out a plan that has appeal, strengthen your relationship with this individual or individuals. Having a mentor for your second life is equally as important as it is for your first.

- Convert some of your future vacations into second-life exploratory adventures. Visit places that could lead to your best second life environment. Check real estate values. Collect data and brochures. Try out different forms of travel. Seek new experiences. View every vacation as an opportunity to enhance both lives.

- Try one new activity each year. Start a list of activities you have always wanted to do but which circumstances did not permit. Learn to swim, play bridge, sail, birdwatch, learn to fly, paint? Start the list now, and then dedicate substantial time to each activity before you start your second life. This will expand your choices when the time comes to formally start a second life. You can reject some ideas now without using up precious time later. Also your first life will improve because of the involvements you are exploring.

Converting promises into goals and goals into reality is not something to do a few months before you retire. Rather, it is a challenge that needs to be addressed as early as possible so you can improve your first life before it is too late.

Think about it.

A SECOND LIFE TIMETABLE

Interviews indicate that most people spend more retirement planning time on financial matters than lifestyle considerations. The attitude these people express is that if they have enough savings and income, lifestyle possibilities will work out automatically. This is not the case. The following chart is designed to help people start balancing financial planning with lifestyle goals early in the planning process.

FINANCIAL TIMETABLE	LIFESTYLE TIMETABLE
Before Age 40	*Before Age 40*
Start contributing to some kind of retirement fund beyond Social Security.	Set up fitness health program to take you into second life in good shape.
Either purchase or begin saving for a home, townhouse, or condo.	Decide if you can carry career into second life or will need a new part-time involvement when the time comes.
Between Age 40-50	*Between Age 40-50*
Verify anticipated Social Security income at age 62 and 65 for planning purposes.	Plan future vacations around a possible second-life living location.
Based on lifestyle plans (opposite), adjust funding to meet goals.	Involve yourself in one new activity (hobby, sport, etc.) each year so you can expand second life options.
Manage IRA and other funds for diversification and maximum earning power.	Study lifestyles of second-lifers in order to discover one or more models.
Between Age 50-60	*Between Age 50-60*
Review status of company or individual pension plan. Adjust for inflation.	Join AARP (American Association of Retired People) and start taking advantages of benefits offered.
Make sure beneficiary designations on insurance policies reflect any changes.	Live three months on your anticipated second life income so you can measure your financial planning with your lifestyle goals.
Review possibilities of starting second life earlier. Set date.	Evaluate your need for a money-making or volunteer involvement in your second life. If necessary, start learning the skills you will need ahead of time.

A SECOND LIFE TIMETABLE (Continued)

FINANCIAL TIMETABLE	LIFESTYLE TIMETABLE
Between Age 60-65	*Between Age 60-65*
Collect documents necessary to process Social Security benefits: proof of both spouses' ages, marriage certificate, etc.	If you are going to relocate, consider purchasing your second-life home in advance.
Weigh merits of waiting until 65 when Medicare kicks in and other benefits occur.	Decide whether you can be happy with a blend of pleasure activities or whether you need some sort of ''mission'' to motivate you in your second life.
Prepare detailed cash flow projections from the date you intend to enter your second life until you reach 90. Take inflation into consideration.	Write out your blueprint for a fulfilling second life and take it to your financial planner to coordinate with financial plans to this point.
One year before starting second life	*One year before starting second life*
If under 65, arrange for a continuation of your medical insurance coverage or, if you are 65, arrange for supplemental Medicare coverage.	If you intend to move into smaller quarters, start shedding personal possessions to simplify your life.
Determine what your pension benefits might be and whether you want to receive them as a lump sum and/or use them to purchase an annuity.	Live a period of six months on your anticipated second life income to verify your financial planning.
Register with Social Security Administration.	If married, do a Plan B in case one spouse is left alone. Increase communications.

Chapter 4
THE MONEY CONNECTION

"In spite of the cost of living, living is still popular."

Anonymous

Have you attended a wedding reception where guests were invited to attach bills to a money tree as a good luck gesture to the bride and groom? In contrast to such an instant and fun money tree, most of us devote our first lives to growing a money tree to take us through our second lives—not only for fun events like vacation trips and special projects, but also possible medical expenses and other contingencies.

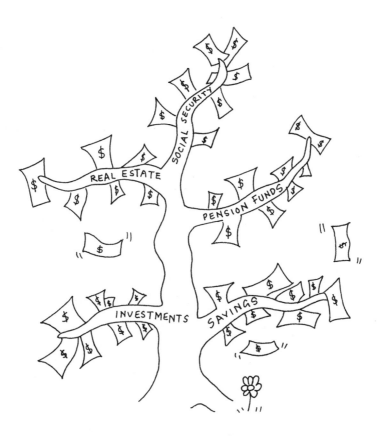

MONEY TREE

Each money tree grows differently, but most money tree plans include Social Security, a pension, some real estate, an investment portfolio, and a form of savings as branches.

When it comes to saving for a second life, everyone has a personal comfort zone. Some feel secure with a modest money tree. Others are motivated to build a much larger one. As a result, some people have too little shade (security) under their tree. Others have more shade that they need. All too few grow a tree designed to accomodate what they really desire in their second lives because they have not planned wisely.

SAVING FOR A DREAM

Most first-lifers figure that if they have enough money on their retirement trees, somehow, things will work out. They refuse to accept that the challenge is not just growing a large tree, but growing one that will accommodate a plan. This means growing a tree the right size for the right plan and then harvesting the money at the right time during one's second life while still saving enough for contingencies. You will learn more about how to accomplish this later in the book.

To get you thinking about the financial planning needed for both lives, please complete the exercise on the facing page.

FINANCIAL EXERCISE

FINANCIAL EXERCISE

(Suggested answers will be found at the end of the quiz.)

TRUE	FALSE	
―――	―――	1. Eighty percent of all assets in America are held by people over 50.
―――	―――	2. Woopies stands for well-off older people.
―――	―――	3. Whether they collect or not, people pay the price for their second lives by saving in their first.
―――	―――	4. Financial planning should not include spending strategies.
―――	―――	5. Most people save money for their second lives without knowing how they will spend it when they get there.
―――	―――	6. One out of ten second-lifers say that their income and savings are adequate.
―――	―――	7. There may be as much emotional security under a modest money tree as a giant one.
―――	―――	8. Over 30 percent work full time after age 65.
―――	―――	9. For most people it is easier to save money in their first lives (automatic withdrawals) than it is to spend it in their second.
―――	―――	10. Sixty-five percent of people expect to earn money working in their second lives.
―――	―――	11. Most people enter their second lives with about 50 percent of their previous income.
―――	―――	12. Inflation is more a factor in one's first life than one's second.
―――	―――	13. The bigger the money tree people grow in their first life, the happier they will be in their second.
―――	―――	14. Certified Professional Financial Planners spend equal time helping clients work out saving and spending strategies.
―――	―――	15. Spouses argue less about spending schedules in their second lives than they do about savings schedules in their first.
―――	―――	16. No two individuals should grow the same kind or size money tree.

ANSWERS: 1. T 2. T 3. T 4. F 5. T 6. F (two out of three say income and savings are adequate.) 7. T 8. F (It is estimated that 10% of people work full time after age 65.) 9. T (many people find the savings habit hard to overcome.) 10. T (only 20% do.) 11. F (70%) 12. F 13. F (this has not been verified.) 14. F (most spend 90% of time on saving strategies.) 15. F (no evidence either way.) 16. T

SCORE ☐

Multiply each correct answer by 6.

If you came up with a score of 70 or above, you are extremely well informed about financial matters. If your score was 50 or above, you are well informed.

FIRST LIFE—SECOND LIFE FINANCIALS

In your first life you earn, save, and manage money. In your second life you manage and spend money. As you study and evaluate the chart below, you can estimate your income and capital accumulation in both lives and decide just what your personal philosophy might be toward spending what you have earned, managed, and saved.

The chart shows how you might earn, manage, and spend money during both lives. The solid line indicates your possible income pattern over a 60-year period. The dotted lines indicate what your capital accumulation curve might look like in your earning years as opposed to your second life or spending years.

HYPOTHETICAL EARNING-SPENDING CHART

Following is an example of an individual who worked 30 years in his first life and lived 30 more in his second life.

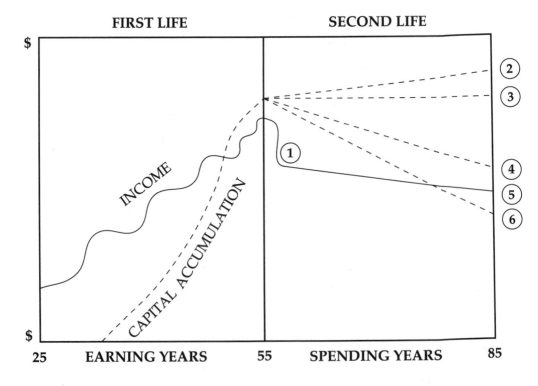

SOME FACTS AND FIGURES

Compare the below items with the corresponding number on the graphic shown on the facing page.

1. Most people enter their second lives with about 70% of their first life income.

2. Some people increase their capital during their second lives by working part-time, not spending income from capital, and/or improving their investment portfolios through skill.

3. Interviews indicate that a surprising number of people add income from capital and spend it but refuse to touch their capital.

4. Some individuals spend a portion of their capital on a preplanned schedule over the various phases of their second lives.

5. Income from Social Security, pensions, and annuities often declines slowly because people spend part of their capital or inflation decreases purchasing power.

6. A few people keep enough for emergencies but are able to end their second lives having spent 50% or more of their original capital. These people learned how to enjoy their income.

WHAT IS YOUR FINANCIAL COMFORT ZONE?

Building a money tree is a complex undertaking. As a guide, three principles are presented. If you agree with a principle, place a check in the appropriate square.

☐ *A Money Tree Is Constantly In Bloom.* Money earns additional money through interest, dividends, and other forms of return. So even if you spend a portion of income-producing capital in your second life, some remains, and it continues to earn or bloom. This makes it possible for you to have your retirement cake and eat it, too. You can enjoy spending some of your capital while that remaining continues to grow. Thus, some of the money on a tree should be viewed as security for contingencies, but some should be considered a spending opportunity to enhance your life.

☐ *Workers Should Nurture A Money Tree That Will Improve Both Lives.* Unfortunately, people build money trees without knowing how they will spend the fruit. To play it safe, they settle for building a big tree (or no tree at all) and postpone any further planning. As a result, some needlessly deny themselves pleasures in their first lives while others, not concerned with growing a tree, leave themselves strapped financially and unable to fully enjoy the many pleasures available in their second lives.

The goal of this principle is to avoid sacrificing the happiness of one life for another because of financial planning. In short, some sort of balance is needed. This can happen only when people are willing to look ahead into their second lives and come up with a fulfillment package that includes specific goals to which a projected price tag can be assigned. This needs to be accomplished early enough to allow people to determine how big a money tree to grow while earning opportunities exist.

☐ *People Should Pick The Fruit From Their Money Tree According To A Schedule.* Once into your second life you may pick too much money at the beginning and be left with too little income later. Or it is possible to be too conservative, and resent it later when you have lost your best opportunities to spend. But how does one know what the future will bring?

More and more people are making plans for their second life based on the expectation they will live longer and move through spending zones.

Obviously, some people want to spend some of their capital for pleasure and fulfillment while their energy levels are high while others never use any of their capital because of the security it provides.

PLAN YOUR FINANCIAL STRATEGY

As you plan your strategy regarding the growth of your money tree and when you intend to pick the blossoms, you may wish to keep the following in mind:

- Some people like to think of money as a flower that only blooms when you spend it on others.

- Small trees can be as beautiful as big trees.

- Modest trees can provide as much security as giant trees.

- You can tell a lot about people by the money trees they grow and when they pick the blossoms.

- Growing a money tree in your first life is more fun when you know for what purpose you will pick the blossoms in your second.

Chapter 5
THE CAREER LINK

> *"Of late I appear to have reached that stage where people look old who are only my age."*
>
> Richard Armour

Looking back, second-lifers often say: "There were a few bumpy spots that I wouldn't want to go through again, but now I am glad that they happened." These people are referring to crisis periods of some kind that caused them to make adjustments and redefine their lives.

Although second-life planning is recommended during both smooth and rough periods, there are three crisis points that might give your planning a big push even though you may not at the time be happy about it. The three crisis periods are:

1. A CAREER CHANGE

Chances are good that sometime during your first life you will be forced, or decide on your own, to seek a *different* career. Should this happen, the bad news is that it could be a major adjustment in your life. *The good news is that it gives you an opportunity to select a career you can take with you into your second life.* Just as there is a money connection between your first and second life, there is also a career link.

Many people work part-time in their second lives. Some do it to augment their income. Others work primarily for psychological reasons. Those who have careers that are easy to carry over into part-time involvements (law, acting, repair work, writing, consulting) usually have an easier transition. Tapering from 40 plus hours per week to around 20 is all that is needed...providing, of course, that this is what is desired. The work preferred is not just a job, it is a mission that provides a purpose for living!

For example, assume you are 50 years of age and the firm where you have been employed as a dispatcher goes into bankruptcy and your job is eliminated. You return to a career center at a local college campus where you narrow down your choices to two: a graphics specialist (you have artistic talent) or a traffic control manager working for a large corporation again. Which choice is best?

If you want to take your new career into a second life where you could work part-time, taking more courses as a free-lance graphic specialist would be your best choice. Translated, those who make career changes (or original choices) in their first lives, should also take into consideration their second lives. Following are two examples:

> When Preston, 46, became disenchanted with his job as a federal employee, he decided to take the money vested in his retirement pension and open a retail picture framing business. He figured that in 10 years he could build the business and sell it for three times as much as his pension would be if he stayed on. This would permit Preston to use his creative talent until he retired and then give him time for his first love—breeding and showing pedigree dogs. In other words, his career decision was made as much upon what he wanted in his second life as in his first.

> Betty lost her job as an office manager at age 52 when her company was taken over by another. Fortunately, she kept her computer skills at a high level so it was easy for her to return to school to take two courses in desktop publishing. This was something she had wanted to do for almost five years. With her new training, she found a job where she would be in charge of publishing a monthly newsletter for employees. Her reasoning was simple. With both training and experience in desktop publishing, she would be in an excellent position to act as a part-time consultant after retirement. Betty understood that critical career changes can be less critical and more motivating when linked to second-life planning.

2. TURNING A MIDLIFE CRISIS INTO AN ADVANTAGE

Although the need for a career switch can precipitate a crisis, other causes exist. For example, there seems to be something about midlife years that causes many people to lose a clear focus on life. The trauma can be accelerated after the last child leaves home, when the aging process of the individual becomes more obvious in the mirror, or when the realization that life is going to be vastly different in the future occurs. Whatever the cause, in making an adjustment, the individual can open the door to second-life planning that will more than compensate for the trauma involved.

> Duke's crisis came when his wife was killed in an automobile accident. The adjustment lasted two years. During this period, Duke made a private search for fulfillment. After receiving an insurance settlement, he decided to quit his regular job and become a counselor. Duke recognized that he could take his new profession into his second life with him on a part-time basis. In fact, it was his primary consideration in making the decision.

> Having separated from her husband soon after graduating from college, Victoria accepted a sales position with a large insurance firm. After two years, knowing she wanted a different career so she could spend more time with her two sons, she attended a support group for single parents. This led Victoria to open an answering service which turned out to be highly successful. When asked what caused her to make the switch, she replied: "I just couldn't look forward to a career with a big company. I decided to make a change early so I could have my cake during my working years and something to keep me involved part-time in my retirement."

3. JUST REACHING A CERTAIN AGE CAN CAUSE CHANGES

Although a personal tragedy or a divorce can move people into career changes, just reaching the age of 40 or 50 can make one take a second look at the future and precipitate some career adjustments. A crisis need not be part of the picture. Most people would like to skip their 40th and 50th birthdays (who needs another reminder?). The good news is that at either of these age junctures, the individual is apt to be in a mood to

As Pam approached her 40th birthday she became extremely sensitive about her age. Although she joined a health club, constantly attempted to improve her wardrobe, and changed hair stylists every few months, she could not maintain her previous upbeat attitude. In discussing the matter with her husband, they decided that an earlier retirement date might benefit both of them. As a result, they developed a sophisticated plan that would allow them to start their second life five years sooner. Within a few months, Pam started to feel better about herself. She had used becoming 40 to help her plan a two-life future. Becoming 50 would be much easier.

Genevieve and Fred (only six months difference in their ages) reached 50. They agreed it was a critical period in their lives. Their three children were on their own. They had reached plateaus in their respective careers. What could they expect of the future? To sort things out, they decided to take a full month vacation at their favorite lake. Away from the pressures of normal living, they made three important decisions. First, they would retire and start their second lives at 60. Second, they would search for a purpose or mission to accomplish in their second lives. Third, they would design a financial plan around the purpose or purposes chosen. Later they agreed that their vacation had been the most enjoyable and productive of any they had ever taken.

Pam, as well as Genevieve and Fred, did not require a career change or a crisis event to force them into a two-life plan, but they *did* capitalize on the turning 40 or 50 syndrome. As it turned out, it was perfect timing.

It is unfortunate that many people must face a traumatic career change or personal crisis to spring them into the possibilities of a second life. Looking back, however, these individuals feel that what they went through was a small price to pay for having the second-life doors opened to them.

A FINAL THOUGHT

One woman interviewed made this comment:

> "It took something highly personal and tragic to jar me into seeing that a second life could be a reality if I planned for it. Once completed, the plan I came up with not only gave me a better future, but is helped me through the crisis period itself."

Individuals, of course, should not wait around to have a crisis or special event spur them into second-life planning. The stakes are too high to place the future into the hands of events over which one exercises limited or no control.

Chapter 6
THE HEALTH BRIDGE

> *"An idea is a feat of association."*
> Robert Frost

Previous chapters have demonstrated the powerful money and career connections between the first and second lives. This chapter will explore additional opportunities. You are invited to express your agreement or disagreement with the ideas presented. To do this, place a ☑ in the appropriate square.

The Health Bridge   Some cars seem to run well with a minimum of maintenance. Then, one day, everything starts to fall apart so you trade the car in on a vehicle in better shape.

Unlike automobiles, you have only one body and you want it to last *two* lives. This means you must give it special care. You don't have the opportunity to pick a better one off a showroom floor. And you can't trade yours in on a new model when it gets old and run down. Like automobiles, your body requires regular upkeep and care, with periodic check-ups.

So why do so many of us allow our bodies and our health to deteriorate needlessly to the point that both our attitude and life expectancy are affected? No one knows. But one thing for sure—most humans, even knowing what is good for them physically, do the opposite.

Have you ever known someone that survived a heart attack to announce upon returning from the hospital that he or she has quit smoking and is going to start exercising and eating right? This is a changed person with a whole new outlook on life. We could say this individual was "scared to health!"

Regular exercise and proper diet must become habits. They must be part of your daily routine. So what great hidden wisdom will motivate you to change your ways? It is simply this: Good health and a positive attitude go hand in hand; if you wish the rewards of a second life, you will want to do all in your power to be *healthy in your first life.*

TWO MEN

Picture two men, Harold and Dave, sitting in a hotel lobby. Harold, obviously overweight, is sitting on the couch and puffing on a cigarette. He is complaining about his present job and career prospects. The second man, Dave, is trim, balding, but well groomed. As Dave stands to leave, he smiles to Harold and assures him that he has a better future than he anticipates. The surprise is that Harold is in his early fifties and Dave is in his seventies!

Harold, unhealthy and out of shape, is unexcited about the future and has given little thought to his second life. Dave, on the other hand, walks two miles a day and is making the most of his second life. Do you see any resemblance between these two men and people you know? Have you noticed that people with a poor outlook on the future often are in poor health?

Do you believe that Harold's negative attitude is the result of being unhealthy, or, do you think on the other hand that Harold's poor state of health is the result of his negative attitude?

The above illustration supports the connection between good health and a positive second-life attitude. If Harold could find a way to develop new hope for his future and a second life, it might cause him to improve his attitude. In turn, this may motivate him to better care for the body he will take into his second life. The health-attitude connection will have been made.

AGREE ☐   DISAGREE ☐

The Activity Bridge   According to Susanne Kunkel, a research director of Scripps Gerontology Center, Miami University, research shows that most people engage in the same limited activities after they leave their full-time careers. Golfers golf, readers read, and ham operators continue to operate. There is nothing wrong with this, but with more free time there is time for a wider range and different blend of activities. In other words, a range of second-life activity involvements should be investigated and started before retirement.

Although you say you have a long list of projects and activities you plan to enjoy in your second life, you probably will, when the time comes, fall back on one or two of your old faithful activities. The answer? Expand your activity involvement now, so you can enjoy them in both lives.

AGREE ☐   DISAGREE ☐

The Balancing Connection   Generally speaking, first life workaholics have trouble reaching a comfortable balance between work, home, and leisure. Home life and leisure activities suffer. As a result, they do not prepare themselves for a fulfilling second life.

> When Mr. Crane was forced to leave his executive position with a major utility, everyone, including his wife, expected him to have trouble. Work had been 90% of his life. Sure enough, being around home bored Mr. Crane. Result? He was almost unbearable to live with until he found another full-time job.

One way to prepare for a rewarding second life (and help your present career) is to learn to balance your career, home, and leisure life now. For many, this is not easy. Yet, most experts agree, achieving a better balance can improve career progress, enhance home life, and make leisure hours more rewarding. The more you learn about balancing in your first life, the more success you will have with your second.

AGREE ☐   DISAGREE ☐

The Sex Continuum   The idea that physical sex plays an insignificant role in one's second life is a major misconception. Sex can be satisfying regardless of a person's age. It is usually not a matter of ability but one of desire, attitude, and opportunity. The more sex is enjoyed at 40, the more it will probably be present at 70 and beyond.

Three factors are involved:

- There are two languages of love. One is physical, the other is companionship and communication. Both can be equally important.

- Having or finding an exciting and cooperative partner plays a key role. Sometimes finding a new partner makes the difference.

- Early attitudes are significant. For some, physical sex is a priority; for others it is balance between the two languages is important. The attitude that one develops early can carry into his or her second life.

AGREE ☐   DISAGREE ☐

The Role Model Connection   Some individuals seem to cope more effectively with growing older that others. These people often work to slow down their aging process (exercise, diet, etc.) but also know how to live gracefully with the process itself. How can you do the same?

It would help if you could locate one or two role models who are enthusiastic and comfortable with what is happening to them in their second lives—a parent, grandparent, friend, neighbor.

> When Marsha suffered job burnout at 53, she was invited to live with her Aunt Helen, who had a large home. Skeptical whether it would work out, Marsha agreed to a trial period. She discovered her aunt, who was 84, had learned how to age with strength and grace. She had pride, friends, and a wonderful philosophy. Within a year Marsha began to model some aspects of her life after Aunt Helen. Result? She decided to live with her aunt permanently.

Some contact with a "master" or "model" senior is recommended because a generational bond can be mutually rewarding.

AGREE ☐   DISAGREE ☐

The Dream Association   Most people find themselves caught up in making money, gaining recognition, and taking care of family responsibilities in their first lives. This does not mean, however, that they do not take time for a few dreams. They do!

The important thing about a dream is that it makes a second life more attractive before you get there. Dreams create expectations. You hear people in their forties and fifties saying: "Sure, I'm trying to satisfy a few dreams on my way to retirement, but I'm so busy I've got to save my big ones until I get there. That is why I am saving so much of my income and getting into investments. When I am finally free of my responsibilities, then watch me fly!"

Many of those who are making the most out of their second lives admit they did "dream planning" in their first. In fact, some hint that without their dreams, both lives would have been dull.

AGREE ☐   DISAGREE ☐

The People Connection   You have probably heard the story of the happily married couple who, in the process of planning their retirement, decided they didn't want to spend it together. The truth, of course, is that the opposite usually happens. It is important, however, to keep one's second life in mind when making commitments to others.

> Single people in their forties and fifties seeking a new partner should keep in mind the "retirement compatibility" factor.

> Couples choosing new living environments should consider the kind of people with whom they will associate.

Making sure you spend a 30-year second life with the right person or people (those within your comfort zone) is critical to good planning.

AGREE ☐   DISAGREE ☐

The Spiritual Connection   Those with strong spiritual beliefs not only maintain positive attitudes in their first lives but build a stronger foundation for their second lives. Verification comes from many sources.

A 30-year-old mother working in a bank: "I expect to experience far more spiritual growth in my second life but the more progress I make now the better prepared I will be then."

An 80-year-old reformed alcoholic: "Tell your readers not to neglect their spiritual side. It will teach them how to live more gracefully with their own advanced aging patterns."

AGREE ☐   DISAGREE ☐

If you agreed with some or all of the above bridges, you have the start of an excellent second-life blueprint.

Chapter 7
CAREER VS FULFILLMENT GAPS

> "When your friends begin to flatter
> you on how young you look, it is a
> sure sign you are getting older."
> Mark Twain

In a typical first life the emphasis is on career success. In a second life the emphasis is more on personal fulfillment. A happy second life is often considered a reward for career success.

IF YOU ARE RIDING HIGH IT IS OKAY TO DELAY
A SECOND LIFE, IF NOT, GO FOR IT!

A career is a time-consuming job or profession that involves productivity for which one is compensated. It is a primary way for people to find a personal identity. Most of us devote years to preparing educationally for a career. Some individuals are so fulfilled with their choices that they postpone second-life pleasures.

Ralph set up a legal practice almost 60 years ago. Now age 84, he shows up each morning at his office. Although younger partners carry the big load, he remains involved. Ralph feels his profession made his first life so rewarding that he has no interest in exploring full-time pleasure possibilities.

Most of us, however, seek some form of self-fulfillment beyond our career-oriented lives. Unlike Ralph, our careers do not *fully* satisfy us. We find ourselves so pressured with first life responsibilities that we are not sufficiently free to fulfill our inner desires. Thus we often save some special adventure, off-beat part-time career, or form of achievement for our second lives. We may work up to an average of 20 hours a week (this, too, can be fulfilling) but we have said good-by to a full-time career.*

---

* Those who continue to work full-time and have Social Security deductions from their salary are, by definition, first-lifers.

No matter how successful we are in our first life, there is a gap between our potential to achieve in our careers and what we actually achieve.

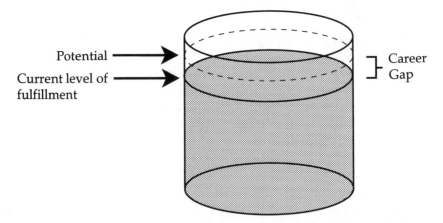

Although each person has different potential, few come close to reaching their true capabilities. When Thomas Edison said, "most people do not come close to their potential," he included himself.

In our second lives, the emphasis usually switches from career to fulfillment. Our potential to achieve is equally as great. Yet, few second-lifers come close to reaching their potential. As the graphic illustrates, pleasure/fulfillment gaps are often dramatically wider than career gaps.

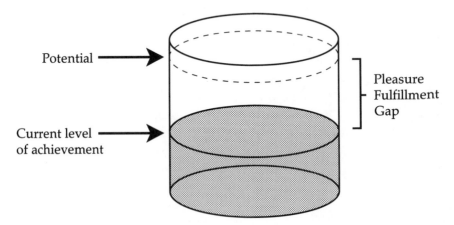

This raises a question. If people live close to their career potential, does this mean they will live close to their fulfillment potential? Does success in one life breed success in the other? Not necessarily.

The illustration below shows four possibilities.

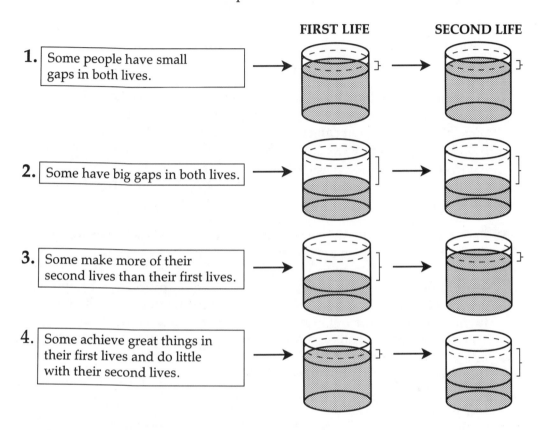

1. Some people have small gaps in both lives.

2. Some have big gaps in both lives.

3. Some make more of their second lives than their first lives.

4. Some achieve great things in their first lives and do little with their second lives.

FIRST LIFE   SECOND LIFE

PLEASURE IS SWEET

Regardless of previous success, those who are serious about designing a plan have the potential to find pleasure, happiness, and fulfillment. Nobody should feel handicapped by first-life mistakes or failures.

Pleasure is sometimes defined as immediate gratification, but it is much more. It is amusement, fun, laughter, and delight. Pleasure may come from the senses or from within. It creates a glow of joy that may last for months. Pleasure can be derived from gardening, listening to music, walking in a park, enjoying a good meal, making love, or doing well at a sport or activity. To some, finding pleasure is what a second life is all about.

FULFILLMENT MAY BE SWEETER

Fulfillment is a deeper kind of satisfaction that comes from reaching a desired goal or dream, living up to a promise, coming close to one's potential or making progress toward spiritual peace.

Fulfillment of any kind leaves a lasting sense of pride and self-worth. Often fulfillment is creative. Usually some degree of recognition is present. But fulfillment can come from reaching the end of a wilderness trail, keeping an attractive home, or contributing to the lives of others on a one-on-one personal basis. Living a long second life is, by itself, a form of fulfillment. One person should never determine what is fulfilling to another.

Pleasure is passing joy while fulfillment restores one's self-esteem and feeds the soul. It brings one closer to the meaning of existence.

Most fulfillment seekers admit they need a serious purpose to balance aspects of their second lives. Some do part-time work because it gives them a feeling of worth. Others gain their sense of purpose from volunteer work. Still others find an inner driving force they are unable to articulate. Sometimes such a force comes from an aspiration or dream they were unable to fulfill during their first lives.

Often the degree to which one can maintain a positive attitude throughout a second life is related to the presence and intensity of a purpose. The stronger the purpose, the easier it is to remain positive. More pleasure and fulfillment are achieved. With the prospect of a 30-year (or longer) second life in good health, the need for finding a suitable purpose or dream goal is greater than ever. Those who plan to retire earlier often are motivated because of a strong inner desire for something not present in their working lifestyles.

Three circumstances often help people close the gap between their current patterns of living and their second life fulfillment potentials.

1. *The Late-Bloomer Syndrome:* Connie Goldman and her audio and video tape programs on successful retirees have popularized the late-bloomer concept. A late-bloomer is a garden-variety individual who seems to lay dormant in life number one and comes into full bloom in life number two. Some of these exciting people may have been restricted in their first lives. With the new freedom that comes with a second life, they spring into action.

   Ted and Maureen led rather dull first lives, but when they met as widow and widower, the chemistry was so good they started going to dances. Both talented musically, they discovered dancing had always been an inner desire that, under their first-life circumstances, had remained unfulfilled.

2. *The Close-Call Premise:* There is some validity to the idea that you need to almost lose something to appreciate and make the most of it. Often, just before or soon after entering a second life, a major health problem causes a person to close the fulfillment gap that was present before the problem occurred.

   Arthur freely admits that his heart attack was responsible for closing his fulfillment gap. ''I was only two years into my second life when it happened, and I was already getting into a rut. Once through recuperation, I realized I was getting a second chance to fulfill some desires I had taken lightly in the past. Although I don't consider myself a religious person, you might say I was 'born again.' ''

3. *The Drastic-Change Theory:* Sometimes a major environmental change is a good way to shock people into closing their fulfillment gaps.

   Gertrude, a recent widow, considered herself fortunate to live in a small town with supportive friends and relatives. But no matter how hard she tried, her life seemed dull. To spring herself loose, she sold her home and started a second life in an adult mobile home park near her sister in another part of the country. Talking about the change, Gertrude said: ''We are all different, but a geographical move was necessary to get me out of my rut and restore my positive attitude. Starting over with new habits and new friends gave me the push I needed.''

THREE QUESTIONS

Ask yourself these questions:

1. Do you want a subdued first life so you can qualify as a late-bloomer in your second?

2. Do you want a health scare to get you to see the potential of your second life?

3. Do you want to gamble with a drastic geographical move in order to motivate yourself?

A second life implies a second chance, and the reader is encouraged to take this attitude regardless of the circumstances she or he faces. The question is—can you afford to wait to get started?

Chapter 8
AMPLE TIME FOR
A FULL SECOND LIFE

> *"Methinks I see the wanton hours*
> *flee, as they pass, turn back and*
> *laugh at me."*
> George Villiers,
> 2nd Duke of Buckingham

Government sources estimated in 1990 that more than two million retirees were seeking part-time work either to supplement their incomes or use up their spare time. This estimate substantiates that most people drastically underestimate the large amount of time available after retirement.

It is further estimated that one out of three second-lifers who do not have part-time jobs would be happier if they did. The figures are even higher for men. This is a signal that in one's second life a part-time job (whether for pay or not) should be viewed more as an activity than a career.

All of this means that when people turn 50, they should get serious about discovering if they are going to need a part-time job to start their second life. If the answer is yes, they need to:

1. Do a second-life *part-time* career search.

2. Prepare ahead of time a strategy (Plan B) to locate and win such a position *before* retirement takes place.*

3. Get some advance experience (moonlighting) in the new career area so that the job will help them through their transition stage.

---

*Elwood N. Chapman is the author of *Be True To Your Future* available through Crisp Publications, Los Altos, California. The book discusses finding the right part-time job (and winning it) while working full-time.

TIME ON YOUR HANDS

It is during the transition into their second lives that most people discover that they have far more time on their hands than anticipated. Why don't people figure this out sooner? Why haven't they factored this time surplus into their planning? Is some form of advance shock necessary? If so, try these figures on for size.

In a 24-hour day, it is estimated that a typical second-lifer who does not work part-time, spends seven hours sleeping and four hours of tasks related to the business of living. Business of living routines include shopping, medical appointments, getting things repaired, preparing and eating meals, housekeeping chores and a host of other things.

This leaves 13 hours each day to be filled!

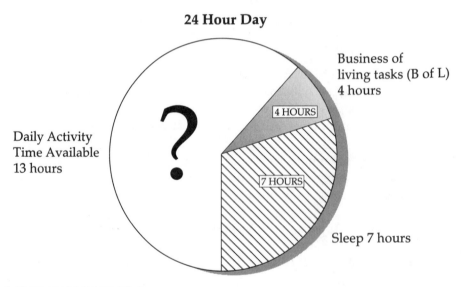

24 Hour Day

Business of living tasks (B of L) 4 hours

4 HOURS

Daily Activity Time Available 13 hours

?

7 HOURS

Sleep 7 hours

ACTIVITY BLENDS

One key to solving this "time on your hands" syndrome is to see that you have the right pleasure/activity mix. You need to discover the blend of involvements that will deliver the highest level of happiness.

All second-lifers have the freedom to place themselves at the activity level that meets their personal values and comfort zones. The amount of pleasure, achievement, and fulfillment they wish to weave into their lives and the way they elect to do it is a personal matter.

Most discover that with so much free time each day and so many years available, designing and updating a blueprint is the way to a happier second life. We will spend more time on this later.

THE TELEVISION TRAP

Television is an insidious time sponge. How much time people allocate to watching television is often a major key to the quality and balance of their lives. As an illustration, Joe Smith devotes seven hours per day to watching television. This is a signal that he is not pursuing many outside activities. Chances are he is not engaging in an adequate health program, or seeking and finding relationships. It isn't that television doesn't provide pleasure, it does. The problem is that it is so accessible it can convert anyone into a "couch potato" at the expense of a more rewarding life. This is bad enough by itself, but the inaction speeds up the aging process instead of slowing it down. As valuable as television may be, it needs to be controlled.

> About three years after Henry left his executive role with a major firm, he found himself watching more and more television at the expense of outside activities. When Henry and his wife took a vacation where television was not available, he got involved in swimming and dancing. To Henry's surprise, he didn't miss television and felt better physically and emotionally. Result? When he got home, Henry cancelled his cable agreement and restricted his television to news and sports. For the first time, he discovered he had a more positive attitude toward other activities and involvements.

No individual should attempt to tell another how to spend his or her free time. The most that can be done is to draw attention to the amount of time available and offer options.

To help you customize a future typical day for yourself, complete the exercise on the next page. It is an excellent way to convince yourself that the challenge is real.

PLEASURE/ACTIVITY MIX EXERCISE

Whether 30, 50, or 80s the diagram below will help you make the best use of your time and, as a result, enhance your second life. Simply fill in the 13 hour space with preferred activities. When a spouse independently completes this same exercise, it is a good idea to match responses and then discuss them. This often will lead to a more compatible mix.

If you prefer working with a weekly schedule on a day by day basis, use the schedule on the following page.

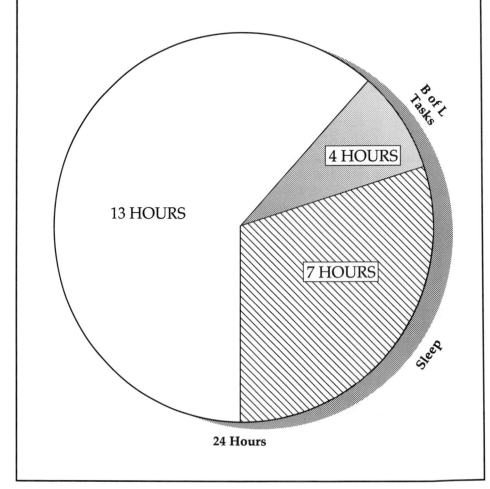

13 HOURS

4 HOURS

B of L Tasks

7 HOURS

Sleep

24 Hours

SECOND LIFE DAILY PLAN

One Day: 24 hours
-7 for sleeping
-4 for the business of living (food preparation, eating, shopping, cleaning, shower, dressing)
—
13 hours

M		T		W		Th		F		SS		
Activity	#Hrs	Activity	#Hrs	Activity	#Hrs	Activity	#Hrs	Activity	#Hrs	Activity	#Hrs	Activity	#Hrs
Breakfast												
Lunch												
Dinner												

Total

Chapter 9
THE ATTITUDE CONNECTION

> *"Never put off till tomorrow what*
> *you do day after tomorrow."*
> Mark Twain

Dr. Ellen J. Langer, in her book *Mindfulness,** makes the following statement:

> *"The notion that the aging process and the physical deteriorization that accompanies it are the inevitable results of the passage of time sets us up for a self-fulfilling prophecy."*

The primary theme of her book communicates that if you fail to outgrow a negative mindset on old age you will become older sooner and not live as long.

Dr. Langer supports her view with considerable research. In one case, the research consisted of an experimental and control group, each with more than 40 individuals. All were residents of the same full-care nursing home. The experimental group was given additional responsibilities such as tending a plant in their rooms, making decisions regarding what to eat, which movie to see, and where to entertain guests who came to visit. In short, they were encouraged to accept more responsibility for their own lives.

Although the control group was given a new plant and activities similar to those of the experimental group, they were told that the staff would take care of things and make the decisions.

A year and a half after the experiment, members of the experimental group were demonstrably more alert, more confident, and less depressed. In short, they seemed to have aged more slowly. Even more dramatic is the fact that during the 18 month interim only half as many in the experimental group had died.

---

*Published by Addison-Wesley Publishing Company, Inc., Reading, Massachusetts

WHAT DOES IT MEAN?

What does it all mean? As Dr. Langer states, when people are involved in making decisions and stretching their minds (mindfulness) they seem to slow down the aging process; when they float along without using their minds (mindlessness) people age faster and, perhaps, die sooner.

To a large extent, mindfulness or mindlessness is an attitude. If you open your mind to the second-life concept, then your chance of having a true, fulfilling second life is enhanced. If you keep your mind closed and continue to cultivate negative images, your years will be less rewarding and more likely there will be fewer of them.

ATTITUDES IMPROVE WITH SECOND-LIFE PLANNING

It is understandable when people in their 40's don't think much about projecting themselves into a second life 10 or more years away. These same people, however, often change their minds when they realize the significant improvements planning can make. Suddenly, second-life planning can become fashionable.

Here are four examples of people who improved their attitudes (and enhanced their destinies) through second life planning. Place a ☑ opposite the case with which you most closely identify.

> ☐ At age 50, Clark and Jenny Cray were approaching retirement without enthusiasm. Then one morning Clark's firm announced that anyone 40 or over was eligible to attend a retirement planning program. Seminars were to be held at night so both Clark and Jenny enrolled. When the seminar was over and they had devoted hours to preparing a plan, Jenny commented: "Without knowing it, Bill and I had grown sour about our respective careers. Then, after some deep searching, we came up with our retirement dream to build a mountain cabin and do some extended traveling. Almost immediately, it did something to our attitudes. Our careers now had a purpose and we got our motivation back. That seminar was the best thing that ever happened to us."

☐ Beverly, a corporate training specialist, was less than enthusiastic when assigned to do preretirement training. She commented: "As if reaching 40 and having my marriage fall apart isn't enough, now I must teach a subject I know little about." But being a professional, Beverly took hold of her new assignment and made the most of it. After leading seminars for a year, she said: "I really enjoy helping people eliminate their fears about retirement. Best of all, it has forced me to plan for myself. As a result, I can see a future I never knew existed."

☐ When Fran and Greg, both 39, took a much needed vacation, they were able to reflect on their deteriorating careers. Fran, a registered nurse, was the first to admit that her attitude needed a boost. Greg talked about organizational conflicts and being boxed in. They both admitted their marriage had been on thin ice for some time. What could they do? They started talking about how long people were living and how a few were making retirement the best part of their lives. Fran talked about how some of her patients said they wished they had planned better for retirement. Before their vacation was over, Fran and Greg made two decisions. First, they would build a retirement plan. Second, they would work harder at their respective careers so they could retire at 50 instead of 60.

☐ Jack found his second-life goal by accident. He was 52 when he lost his wife to illness. The discovery came about when a neighbor, hoping to help him with his loss, invited Jack on an RV trip. Jack discovered three things. First, he enjoyed the lifestyle. Second, his mechanical skills enabled him to help others with their RV's. Third, the wanderlust in him came to the surface.

When Jack returned to work he discovered that he was motivated to pay his back bills, mortgage on his home, and save for an RV. Result? Jack was able to begin planning for a second life.

In all four cases, second life planning created an attitude "turnaround" beneficial to both lives.

SECOND LIFE PLANNING CREATES A HEALTHY MIND

Shelly Taylor in her excellent book *Positive Illusions: Self-deception and the Healthy Mind** deals with future planning in an unusual manner. Her comments:

"Normal people believe to an unrealistic degree that the future holds a bounty of good things and few bad things. Depressed people are more realistic."

Most of us are guilty to some degree of self-deception as far as the future is concerned. This is especially true of those who do positive second-life planning.

This book encourages this attitude for these reasons:

- A positive bias (perception) can shelter one from the harsher side of reality and bring greater fulfillment.

- Rechanneling negative incoming information in positive directions enhances our ability to cope with life and increases mental health.

- An optimistic view of future events improves life today and, if it doesn't go too far, makes reality easier to cope with when it arrives.

It is my firm belief that in order to find maximum pleasure and fulfillment now (whatever your age) you must view the long-term in a positive way. This should be done with an awareness of reality; but for planning purposes, positive factors should be played up and the negative down. In short, when you force yourself to see the best, you are on a winning track.

Basic Books, Sub-Division, Harper & Rowe Publications, 10 E. 53rd Street, New York, NY 10022, 1989

Chapter 10
THE CONTINGENCY WHEEL

> *"Man blames fate for other accidents,*
> *but feels personally responsible when*
> *he makes a hole in one."*
>   Horizons Magazine

Entering into a second life without a positive attitude can be like taking an expensive vacation you didn't want to take in the first place. Nothing will go right. Within a few days you start talking about what has gone wrong, not what is going *right*. Soon your negative attitude has traveled to others and before long everyone is looking forward to the end of the vacation. When traveling it is more important to remember your positive attitude than your travelers checks.

This does not mean, however, that a positive attitude will make things go smoothly. You can still have flight delays, bad weather, or illness. What it *does* mean is that you will handle such problems in a better way and still get pleasure and fulfillment out of the experience.

As with a vacation, you should factor in the possibility of unforeseen conditions into your second life. Your positive attitude is essential, but it won't eliminate all of the bumps in your journey. The contingency wheel includes six major adjustments that might be required. All are applicable to both lives.

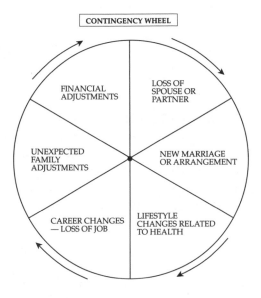

CONTINGENCY WHEEL

FINANCIAL ADJUSTMENTS

LOSS OF SPOUSE OR PARTNER

UNEXPECTED FAMILY ADJUSTMENTS

NEW MARRIAGE OR ARRANGEMENT

CAREER CHANGES — LOSS OF JOB

LIFESTYLE CHANGES RELATED TO HEALTH

CONTINGENCY WHEEL

FINANCIAL ADJUSTMENTS

LOSS OF SPOUSE OR PARTNER

UNEXPECTED FAMILY ADJUSTMENTS

NEW MARRIAGE OR ARRANGEMENT

CAREER CHANGES — LOSS OF JOB

LIFESTYLE CHANGES RELATED TO HEALTH

LOSS OF SPOUSE OR PARTNER

Although a plan should take into consideration all contingencies, special attention should be given to the possibility that one spousal member might find it necessary to go it alone. Although the ratio of married women over 65 who are left alone is 3 to 1 over men, each member should have a plan developed and discussed along with the master blueprint.

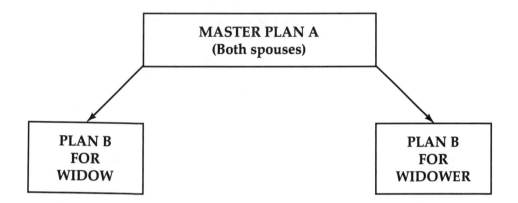

In the development of contingency Plan B's, the following suggestions are made:

- The remaining spouse should be left with a financial plan agreed to in advance after provisions for legal fees, taxes, and any distribution of funds through a will or trust.

- Trust funds for children, grandchildren, and others should be a part of master plan.

- Frequent and open communications regarding changes and progress of plan is a must.

- Both parties should have access to all financial data.

- After mutually agreed upon distribution of funds upon the death of another, each party should have full freedom to develop his or her own Plan B. Under ideal circumstances, each partner can play the role of consultant to the other.

FLEXIBILITY AND CONTINGENCIES

How can one develop flexibility to cope with either first- or second-life contingencies? How can one prepare a plan that can be adjusted to changes that cannot be anticipated in advance? One idea is to create a plan that is more a package of possibilities than something written in cement—more like a living trust that can be changed to meet new situations rather than an irrevocable trust that cannot. Or, if you prefer, a plan that grows as you meet new situations.

A second idea is to practice flexibility now so that it becomes a habit. What this often means is adjusting to disappointments—switching to a new career path when the one you preferred closes—adjusting your financial strategy to meet new conditions—and accepting change as a challenge instead of a defeat.

Here are three additional suggestions.

1. Accept change as an alternate avenue leading to even greater fulfillment. Some people see change as a monster that will upset their lives. Others view change as a caterpillar that will slowly eat up what they love most; but it remains possible to focus on any change as a butterfly that will bring moments of beauty and fulfillment. Can you train yourself to adopt this serendipitous attitude?

2. Enjoy the past, but avoid comparing the way life is today to what it was years ago. For example, many of us in our second lives make the mistake of trying to get our adult children to live the kind of life we led years ago *when times were different*. This does not work. The world is changing, society is changing, neighborhoods are changing—all of us are on a conveyor belt leading us into a different world. Reflecting on the past is pleasurable and recommended, but looking ahead to the future in a positive way (watching history unfold) is the attitude that helps us deal with contingencies should they arrive.

3. Travel lighter. Some people enter their second lives dragging so many possessions, prejudices, and worn-out relationships with them that they never overcome the handicap. There is nothing wrong with fighting to keep your own home, your many personal possessions, your animals, and some of your previous habits—but if the luggage weighs you down and results in a negative attitude, the price is too high.

Chapter 11
PRACTICAL COPING TECHNIQUES

> *"Life can only be understood backwards, but is must be lived forwards."*
>
> Soren Kierkegaard
> (1813-1855)

This chapter discusses common attitudes that help others make more of their lives. They manifest themselves in simple expressions that, to some, have considerable merit. Please read the chapter and prioritize the list by writing the number 1 in the box opposite the technique that has the most meaning and therefore could give you the most help. Continue this process until you have written a 5 in the space opposite the idea that has the least meaning to you.

☐ **"I HAVE LESS TO LOSE"**
The idea here is to convince yourself that no matter where you are in either life, you are *already a winner*. For example, if you are 50 and well on your way to reaching your career goal, you can start viewing your first life as a success and, with a victory already behind you, consider yourself in a bonus situation. This is like winning big in roulette and then enjoying yourself on "winnings." Martin reflects this cavalier attitude.

> "Why should I lose my spirit and confidence with only 10 years left to work? I've already won the first game. I'm going to get a couple more promotions, increase my retirement income, and then make the most of my new freedom. What have I got to lose?"

☐ **"IT'S NOT OVER UNTIL IT'S OVER."**
This Yogi Berra phrase, frequently used by coaches when their teams are far behind, fits both lives. Many do not reach their financial goals until late in their first lives. They struggle until the whistle blows. But, once accomplished, they have great second-life attitudes because they know the game is just starting. Mrs. Bailey expresses this upbeat attitude.

> "I go for the two life idea because it has goal-setting possibilities. Like in a basketball game, I'm going to do my best in each life and keep telling myself that the game isn't over until I've led two fulfilling lives."

☐ **"ATTITUDE RENEWAL IS MY ACE IN THE HOLE."**

Those who recognize that a positive attitude requires a frequent overhaul wisely view every phase in both lives as a new challenge. This view helps them forget past mistakes and start over. Regardless of how much time they have spent on a master plan, they design a new strategy for each phase or zone. Many make the process of renewal a weekly, monthly, and annual process. Mrs. Drake perceives attitude renewal in this way.

> "To me renewal is restoration. You rebuild yourself for the next chapter in life. I like the two life concept; but knowing me, I would probably divide each life into smaller sections so that renewal would be more frequent. This way I would always be starting over without limitations. As you can tell, I am a highly goal-oriented person. Unless I have a short-term goal to reach, I lose my positive attitude."

☐ **"I INTEND TO BEAT THE ODDS"**

The thought here is to try and beat published life-expectancy figures (see page 7). Once you know the odds, you start taking care of your body in your first life so that you can beat the tables in your second. Those who recommend this attitude know that when they are 50 it may be more important to work-out regularly than it is to put money into a retirement account.

You need not be a gambler to assume this strategy—just be stubborn and disciplined. When you recognize the long time span and successive opportunities within a second life, you are motivated to enter it in the best possible shape. For example, the best time to stop smoking is in your first life, not your second. Rose has demonstrated the value of this practical attitude.

> "Like other people my age, I read the obituaries. When I see I have outlasted others I feel good because I know I am hanging in there. It motivates me to continue my good health practices and routine. Tell your young readers that all the money they spend in health spas and on exercise equipment is a good idea. It's fun to beat the odds."

☐ "DESTINY IS ON MY SIDE."

There is a touch of the metaphysical to this strategy. You hear these comments.

> "I'm not going to worry about how long I live. I'm just going to make the most of every day until my number comes up."

> "Longevity may be in my genes but I'm not going to flirt needlessly with fate."

> "I have a lucky star and, as long as I pay my human rent, it will continue to shine."

It doesn't matter why or how people enhance their life expectancies, dispel their doubts, and keep their positive attitudes—just so it happens! Gus takes this view.

> "I'm years away from retirement, but as long as I have God as my co-pilot, I'll welcome each stage as it comes. My wife and I are going to do the best job of planning we can manage; but when we make our transition into a second life, a higher power will still be our navigator."

To each his own. The important thing is coming up with a system or technique that keeps one up instead of down. Those who live out their first lives with high self-esteem may find it easier to use the same techniques to extend their success formulas into their second lives. Most people, however, will require some new approaches.

Chapter 12
A SECOND LIFE IS
NOT FOR SISSIES

> *"I refuse to admit I'm more than fifty-two even if that does make my sons illegitimate."*
>
> Lady Astor

Are you willing to throw away your preconceived ideas about what really happens in retirement? Are you ready for a revolutionary view? Are you prepared to take risks? If so, get ready for the five-zone approach!

It is only natural to be cautious about a departure from accepted doctrine. When I first introduced the idea of breaking retirement into parts, my friends showed little enthusiasm. Some have changed their minds.

Four years ago I had an extended discussion about the idea with a close friend who reviews my preliminary manuscripts. He was critical and wary, saying the five phases sounded contrived. Last month we had a second discussion, and I noticed a change in his attitude. "You know," he said, "I find myself charting my second life according to the five stages you identified. A big plus is that I do not fear growing old as much. I used to think it would be best not to know what lies ahead. Now I'm not so sure. When I am 75 and can still look ahead to different levels of fulfillment, it is far better than a straight line or too much of the same thing. You may have something after all."

We are acquainted with the traditional phases and transition periods most people go through in their first lives. We have been slow to recognize, however, that a similar process may occur in our second lives. The illustration on the next page encourages this comparison.

THE FIVE PHASES OF TWO LIVES

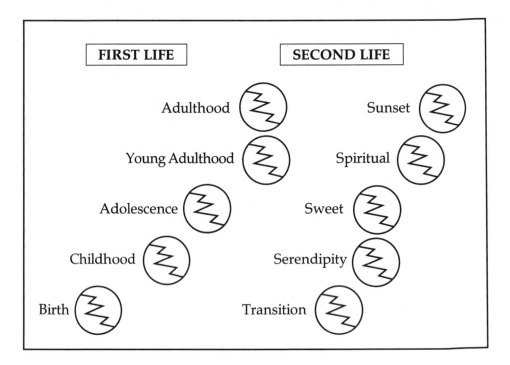

Please notice the similarities:

- All phases move in an upward, positive direction.

- No time period is specified.

- The wavy lines inside each circle remind us that moving into a new phase takes time and may require a few "in and back" movements. They also represent the doubts and loss of identity that can take place in making a passage to the next phase.

Although using terms such as "stages" and "phases" communicates that a second life is divided into parts, it is more accurate to use the term "zones." A zone implies an enviroment where individuality is permitted. It also implies that for maximum pleasure and fulfillment, each individual must make adjustments to become comfortable within each zone. Where a stage and phase can signify a definite beginning and ending; zones meld into each other without firm lines of demarcation. The illustration on the facing page provide a better picture.

THE FIVE ZONES*

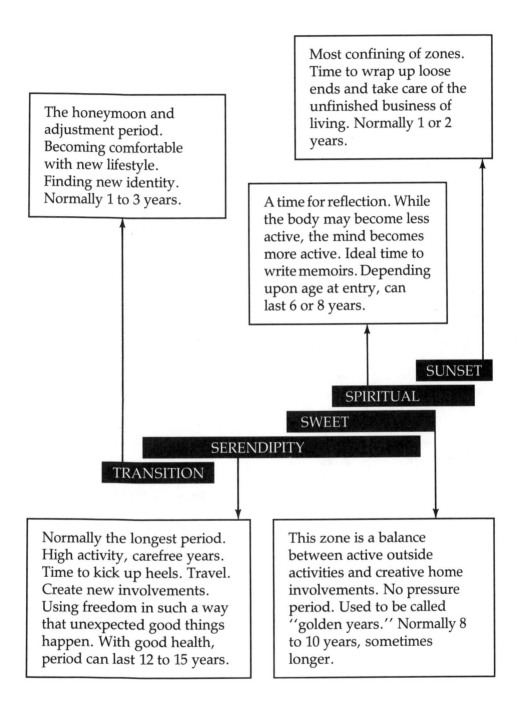

Most confining of zones. Time to wrap up loose ends and take care of the unfinished business of living. Normally 1 or 2 years.

The honeymoon and adjustment period. Becoming comfortable with new lifestyle. Finding new identity. Normally 1 to 3 years.

A time for reflection. While the body may become less active, the mind becomes more active. Ideal time to write memoirs. Depending upon age at entry, can last 6 or 8 years.

SUNSET

SPIRITUAL

SWEET

SERENDIPITY

TRANSITION

Normally the longest period. High activity, carefree years. Time to kick up heels. Travel. Create new involvements. Using freedom in such a way that unexpected good things happen. With good health, period can last 12 to 15 years.

This zone is a balance between active outside activities and creative home involvements. No pressure period. Used to be called ''golden years.'' Normally 8 to 10 years, sometimes longer.

*See Book III for additional information.

THE FIVE ZONES

As you study the five zones, please notice:

- As in the illustration on page 64, the zones are arranged to indicate upward movement where new, positive challenges exist.

- The zones overlap so that an individual is free to lengthen one zone and shorten another. Some people the same age move into another zone years ahead of others.

- The longer one zone is stretched, the shorter others become. It is natural for those in good health to stretch beginning zones.

- Moving into a new, higher zone implies an adjustment.

- The later zones provide pleasures and fulfillments not available in earlier ones.

- As a general rule, when the zone ahead shows promise of providing more comfort and fulfillment, it is time to consider moving into it.

CONTINUED GROWTH WITHIN EACH ZONE

Most people have a mind-set that they will grow to maturity and then live out their lives adjusting to diminishing capacities. These individuals find it difficult to accept:

Mini-trajectories: This means that one's second life can be divided in parts where new growth can continue within each part even though one becomes older with each advance. The linear mindset—that life is a straight line that slowly turns downward at the end—prevails.

Continuous development.   This suggests it is possible to compensate or offset lower physical capacities with an increase in mental growth. Aging, to these people, has come to refer to the negative side of growing older, which eliminates the possibility of growth in a new direction. They reject the idea that the mind can pick up the slack when the body slows down.

BENEFITS FROM TAKING ONE ZONE AT A TIME

The benefits of a five-step approach over one long linear stage are many. Following are seven.

BENEFIT 1. The Zones Do Not Restrict You. People tend to become more individualistic in their second lives, so they reject a computerized journey. Considerable freedom of movement is appreciated and desired. Although the primary force that moves people into the next zone is aging, one is free to return to a previous zone if health permits. It is also possible for married couples to be happy living most of the time in different zones, providing they understand what is happening. Give each other space, and communicate frequently.

BENEFIT 2. The Planning Advantages Are Significant. The five zones constitute a roadmap around which you can build a second life plan. Like viewing a map, if you don't know your destination and what lies in between, you do not know how to deal with the challenges that exist in the beginning.

Those who perceive retirement as a straight line are more apt to give up on their planning because of boredom. When different opportunities lie around the next bend, the same people can become involved. It is also easier to design five small plans that can be adjusted and woven into a master plan than it is to become frustrated by biting off more than you can chew.

BENEFIT 3. The Five Zones Facilitate Financial Planning. Once you understand the possibilities within each zone, you can determine approximately how much of your income and capital you intend to spend within each. For example, a single person with substantial capital could decide to spend 10% in the Transition Zone, 40% in the Serendipity, 20% in the Sweet, and save the rest for contingencies. Without zones or stages, this kind of financial planning is impossible.

BENEFIT 4. You Know Which Activities To Save For Later Zones. You can select those activities to engage in early (dancing, cycling) and those to save (waltzing, walking) until later. Activity spreading can be the key to a more pleasurable second life. Zoning makes this possible.

BENEFITS FROM TAKING
ONE ZONE AT A TIME (Continued)

BENEFIT 5. Better Major Decisions Can Be Made. This may be the number one advantage to zoning. For example, at what time might it be best to move into a retirement or life-care center? Would it be best at the beginning or the end of the Sweet Zone? Guideposts are needed for many kinds of major decisions. Zoning provides a reference point.

BENEFIT 6. Communication Is Improved. Those who divide their second life into progressive zones communicate better during the planning stage and when adjustments are required later. Communication between spouses is especially important during early planning stages if a mutually rewarding plan is eventually designed. What should we plan for the Serendipity Zone? What should we save for the Sweet Zone? How much of our capital should we save until we reach the Spiritual Zone? Without guideposts, communications are difficult. Broken down into five stages, communications can be fun and rewarding.

BENEFIT 7. Zones Provide Replanning Junctures. Just as there are passage points in a first life, major adjustments are sometimes called for in a second life. For example, someone in the Serendipity Zone might be encouraged to move more quickly into the Sweet Zone because of a serious illness. Moving from one zone to another requires new planning and adjustments. Knowing when this should take place and what to plan for is critical. Having zone junctures helps people restore their positive attitudes and get a new lease on life.

SPECIAL CONSIDERATIONS

There are many additional advantages to the zone system of viewing a second life. Others will surface as you study the individual zones in the chapters ahead. In doing this, please keep the following in mind:

- With health as the big question mark, no specific time periods can be assigned to the five zones. You may wish, however, to predict how much time you may spend in each period. For example, if your life expectancy figure indicates you can anticipate 30 years in your second life, you can divide the time among the five zones for planning purposes. If it should turn out the way you anticipate, you will have enjoyed a full second life. If your health should deteriorate along the line, you might need to compress the time you spend in remaining zones. Your planning will still have been valuable.

- In the long run, neither couples nor singles have a planning advantage. Although the planning process may be more fun between two compatible people, those who plan alone eliminate the need to compromise.

- A positive attitude is a psychological advantage that stacks the deck in favor of winding up with a superior blueprint and then putting it into operation. It is critical that each zone be anticipated. Without a positive attitude, this will probably not happen.

- The five zones were selected on the basis of interviews, observation, and previous writings. My publication, *The Unfinished Business of Living**, was especially helpful. Although the five zones came from many people, there is nothing to keep you from adding or subtracting from the number of zones, or changing a zone to suit your own individual interpretation.

- As any individual progresses through the different zones, behavioral changes will take place. The aging process will be responsible for many changes, but not all. Some will occur because of preference and attitude. The reader is encouraged to match behavioral characteristics listed in each zone with those of others who may have reached that zone. This may encourage a small degree of intergenerational understanding and mutual appreciation.

*Published by Crisp Publications, Inc. 95 First Street, Los Altos, California 94022

Chapter 13
MAKING THE MOST
OF BOTH LIVES

> *"Age is not all decay; it is the ripening, the swelling, of the fresh life within, that withers and bursts the husk."*
>
> George Macdonald

The song with the title that asks the question "What's it all about, Alfie?" reminds us that, at times, we all search for meaning, purpose, or significance in our existence. We try to probe beyond our daily view of reality.

During these moments, we seek a higher dimension of thought that might make what we are doing seem more important. If possible, we want a glimpse of our own mortality. Regardless of our age, most of our searching results in frustration. On rare occasions, however, a little light shines through. When this occurs, we are encouraged to move into the future with more vigor.

It is natural and to be expected that when people start to design a second life plan, their search for fulfillment intensifies. Because of this, an attempt has been made in this book to point out a few road signs that can lead to new and rewarding meanings. In presenting these views, I am indebted to Dr. Victor F. Frankl, the founder of Logotherapy, who, through his book *Man's Search for Meaning* (New York, N.Y.: Washington Square Press, 1959) and more recent publications, has made a most significant contribution.

Please ☑ whether you agree or disagree with the following statements.

FULFILLMENT IN ONE'S FIRST LIFE IS OFTEN INDEPENDENT OF SUCCESS AS KNOWN AND ENJOYED IN ONE'S SECOND LIFE.
Career success, and the power, recognition, and money that go with it, may be the primary measuring stick in one's first life. Inner fulfillment may be the primary reward in one's second life. Some executives have more difficulty finding fulfillment than the custodians that worked for them.

AGREE ☐   DISAGREE ☐

SPIRITUAL NEEDS INCREASE IN ONE'S SECOND LIFE.
This is not caused by the aging process alone but because we have the time to search and reflect. Living out a first life with little meaning is distressing enough, living out a second life without some form of spiritual uplift is like watching an outstanding television drama without sound. The action may keep us occupied but the meaning is lost.

AGREE ☐ DISAGREE ☐

WORK HAS MEANING. To many people, achieving work goals brings fulfillment. This is why many continue to work on a limited basis in their second lives. Those who recognize the value of work and continue to be involved into second life zones are to be respected as long as they balance it with other activities and fulfillments not possible in their first lives.

AGREE ☐ DISAGREE ☐

THE RICHER YOUR LIFE EXPERIENCES, THE CLOSER YOU COME TO THE DISCOVERY OF MEANING. Although insights and wisdoms are available in both lives, it is the blending of both lives that can create a man or woman for all seasons. Personal growth opportunities are equally available in both lives.

AGREE ☐ DISAGREE ☐

THE STAND YOU TAKE TOWARD YOUR OWN FATE IS CRITICAL.
For example, should you become ill, it would be your attitude toward overcoming the illness that could lead you to a new dimension of meaning.

AGREE ☐ DISAGREE ☐

THE JOY OF GIVING. Many people discover that there is an inner fulfillment that comes from the joy of sharing time and possessions. The ideal time to do this is in one's second life.

AGREE ☐ DISAGREE ☐

THE DEFIANT SPIRIT: In some of his writings, Frankl refers to the "defiant power of the human spirit." For example, those who do everything possible to resist their own aging process can be said to have such a spirit. It can also be observed in many other situations.

The coach who suffers a humiliating defeat one season and wins the championship game the next.

The individual who finally makes a marriage work the third time around.

The 90-year-old widow who refuses to leave her free-standing home to live in a retirement center.

Defiance, it would appear, can lift the human spirt. If not carried too far, it is a characteristic to be admired and provides a way of coping as well as a philosophical attitude.

AGREE ☐ DISAGREE ☐

ONE'S DESTINY CAN BE ENHANCED. Whatever the circumstances that an individual faces in the future, the level of pleasure and fulfillment available can be enhanced with a positive attitude. All some people see in the winter of their second life is a stubble of grain left over from the spring, summer, and fall plantings. They ignore the granary (silo) where all of the grain (memories) is stored. Even though their lives have been full, they look only at the stubble.

Then there are those who focus on the granary *but it is not full*. These positive individuals are still looking ahead to future harvests. They want to make more memories to store in the granary.

I would like to be a member of this group—to perceive existence as a silo that can never be filled no matter how long one may live.

AGREE ☐ DISAGREE ☐

CLOSING SUGGESTIONS

1. Enhance your destiny by anticipating more pleasure and fulfillment from an experience than is realistic to expect.

2. View each phase in your first life and each zone in your second life as a separate journey, each with unique growth opportunities.

3. Whatever your age, recognize that success or failure in the next stage is primarily dependent upon your attitude.

4. Your primary challenge is to learn how to live in harmony with your aging process—this applies whether you are 30-something or 70-something.

5. Live each phase or zone through as though it were the last; but, when the time comes, accept the next period with enthusiasm.

6. Accept the premise that making a passage from one phase or zone to another can be traumatic for yourself, your children, and your parents.

7. Make a magnificent effort to find your own comfort level within each zone but do not become so comfortable you are fearful of new experiences and adventures.

8. Be disciplined about maintaining your mental and physical health.

9. Whatever the two-life philosophy you eventually design for yourself, refer to it often so that your positive attitude doesn't slip away from you.

10. Every once in awhile (on your birthday?) give yourself a party to celebrate the success you are experiencing in your own aging process.

BOOK II

SECOND LIFE
PLANNING GUIDE

"Retirement, for most people, is getting away from the frustrations of a job they no longer like, not going toward something important."

Phillip G. Yuhas

HOW TO USE BOOK II

This practical, self-paced guide is designed as a supplement to Book I. Field testing indicates that to make the best use of the guide two conditions are desirable.

- The reader should have fully digested Book I and although approval to all ideas is not anticipated, the stronger the commitment to the two life philosophy the better.

- Spouses should work as a team and, where necessary, make compromises on a page by page basis.

With pencil in hand, please follow these suggestions:

- Answer all questions as you go, even though you may return and make changes later.

- In answering questions, take your personal comfort zones into consideration.

- How you manage and spend your available funds is a critical part of second-life planning. The closer you come to writing down actual figures the better, *but rough estimates are acceptable.*

Once completed, this guide constitutes the basic blueprint for an exciting second life. Similar to a will or living trust, changes will need to be made, but the guide becomes the framework for the future.

INTRODUCTION

Charles Champlin, arts editor of the *Los Angeles Times*, recently started an upbeat article on our new decade in this manner: "Like birthdays, years divisible by 10 have a special aura about them. In the case of private birthdays, the aura gets darker and darker as the numbers go up. Turning 50 has a chill about it, like a cloud passing the face of the sun, and let us not speak of 60 at all."

The best way to remove clouds of depression that often go with becoming 40, 50, or 60 is to plan for a longer life. If you plan a rewarding second life that can easily last 30 years, you gain a new perspective about earlier birthdays. You joyfully realize that being 40, 50, or 60 simply demonstrates growth achievement for those periods with many stages remaining. This perspective can make you feel much better about your present age.

This guide has been prepared to help you enhance your destiny in practical, step-by-step manner. There are four parts.

PRELIMINARY PROJECTIONS

QUESTIONS

1. Is 30 too young to explore the possibilities of a second life?

   Yes ☐   No ☐

2. What year do you intend to start your second life?

   Year _____

3. What age would you like to achieve in your second life?

   Age _____

4. Are you negative about your years after 60?

   Yes ☐   No ☐   Undecided ☐

5. Do you accept the premise that a strategy is necessary to make the most out of your second life?

   Yes ☐   No ☐   Undecided ☐

6. Has the term "second life" started to replace the R word in your vocabulary?

   Yes ☐   No ☐

7. Do you feel your second life prospects are good enough to start improving your health now?

   Yes ☐   No ☐   Undecided ☐

8. Are you denying yourself too much now in order to build a big nest egg later?

   Yes ☐   No ☐   Undecided ☐

9. Do you intend to make the attitude connection? That is, develop a strategy good enough to improve your present attitude?

   Yes ☐   No ☐   Undecided ☐

10. Will you need a part-time job or substantial volunteer involvement in your second life?

    Yes ☐   No ☐   Undecided ☐

PRETEST

This exercise has been designed to refresh your memory on some of the basic concepts presented in Book I and to better prepare you to complete this guide. Answers to the true and false questions are provided on the following page.

True **False**

____ ____ 1. Most people pass up the rewards of a second life because they have a negative mindset toward retirement.

____ ____ 2. Planning for a second life does not enhance your first life.

____ ____ 3. People pay for their second life during their first life but seldom cash in.

____ ____ 4. Trivialization of one's second life is uncommon.

____ ____ 5. Completing this guide can have immediate benefits.

____ ____ 6. There is no connection between your first-life career and fulfillment in your second life.

____ ____ 7. There are only two things a person can do in their first life (save money, improve health) that will impact on their second life.

____ ____ 8. Most people have little trouble finding challenging things to do in their second lives.

____ ____ 9. Few second lives last more than 20 years.

____ ____ 10. Dividing a second life into zones makes it easier to do successful planning.

____ ____ 11. Experiencing growth in all five zones is impossible.

____ ____ 12. One should stretch his or her Serendipity Zone as far as possible without taking anything away from future zones.

____ ____ 13. A positive attitude is more important in one's first life than one's second.

True	False	
____	____	14. What one does with one's first life has little to do with second-life fulfillment.
____	____	15. In making the most out of the five zones, the Sweet Zone is the least difficult.
____	____	16. A positive attitude can tip destiny in your direction.
____	____	17. Each member of a marriage should have a Plan B to supplement their master plan.
____	____	18. "Beat the Odds" is an example of a practical philosophy.
____	____	19. The granary idea is a conceptual philosophy that uses a silo as a metaphor.
____	____	20. Success in your first life guarantees success in your second.

TOTAL CORRECT [   ]

A score of 15 to 20 indicates you have carefully read the book *Enhance Your Destiny* and have developed a sound concept toward the possibilities of a full and exciting second life. A score under 15 may be a signal that you would benefit from spending more time with the text and retake this pretest a second time.

ANSWERS: 1. T 2. F 3. T 4. F 5. T 6. F (It is a good idea to select a career that is easy to take into one's second life). 7. F (The book lists many other connections) 8. F (Not finding a challenge is the biggest tragedy of a second life). 9. F (The average is closer to 30 years). 10. T 11. F 12. T 13. F 14. F 15. F (most difficult to gain a balance) 16. T 17. T 18. T 19. T 20. F

BOOK II

PART 1

FINANCIAL PLANNING

IT'S SMART TO START EARLY

Ideally, investing for your second life should begin early, often when you can least afford it. Buying a home, starting a family, and just trying to meet expenses can put retirement planning far down on your priority list. But there is no better time to capture the benefits of compounded earnings than in your early working years—when time is on your side. Even a small amount of capital invested each month can grow significantly if it has many years to compound.

This illustration reflects the growth of a hypothetical investment of $100.00 per month at an assumed 10% rate of return. Growth with simple interest and with monthly compounded interest are compared.

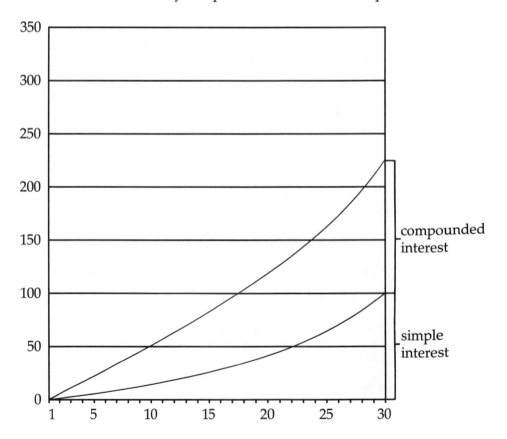

Financial planners today estimate you will need around 75% of your income at retirement to enjoy a pleasurable and fulfilling second-life style. While costs for housing, clothing, and other family expenses may decline in your second life, the rising cost of health care may offset these savings.

To calculate the estimated monthly income you will need—in tomorrow's dollars—you must factor in a projected annual inflation rate for the number of years between now and when you start your second life. Here is how to figure what you will need.

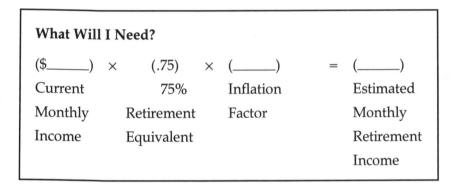

What Will I Need?

($_____) × (.75) × (_____) = (_____)
Current 75% Inflation Estimated
Monthly Retirement Factor Monthly
Income Equivalent Retirement
Income

For example, let's assume you are earning a monthly income of $4,000 (before taxes) and you want to have a $3,000 monthly income (75% equivalent) when you commence your second life. With a 5% inflation rate over the next 10 years, that would mean you would need $4,890 monthly ($3,000 × 1.63) at retirement to match the buying power of $3,000 today. And that monthly figure does not account for a change in your tax rate. Of course, it is anticipated that your monthly income will continue to increase.

Inflation Factor		
(Assumes average long-term inflation rate of 5%)		
	Year of Retirement	
Current Age	**(Age 65)**	**Inflation Factor**
62	1994	1.16
60	1996	1.28
55	2001	1.63
50	2006	2.08
45	2011	2.65
40	2016	3.39
35	2021	4.32

Now that you have calculated what your second-life income need will be, you must decide how to develop sufficient resources to meet that need. With the help of your local Social Security office and your company's benefits department, you can get a good fix on what your current benefits would provide you. When you add to that an estimated monthly income from your personal investments, you will come up with an estimate of the total monthly income you will be able to draw upon to fulfill your second-life goals.

How Much Will I Have?

	Estimated Monthly Retirement Income
Social Security	$ _____
Company Pension	$ _____
Investment Portfolio	$ _____
Stocks	$ _____
Bonds	$ _____
Mutual Funds	$ _____
IRAs	$ _____
Annuities	$ _____
Savings	$ _____
Life Insurance	$ _____
Other	$ _____
Total Estimated Monthly Retirement Income	$ _____

After you have calculated the difference between the income you will need and the resources you will have to draw upon, you may find that there is a significant gap between your needs and assets. And don't forget, in addition to your income you should decide how much capital you need for special goals and emergencies. That is why early financial planning and building an investment portfolio is suggested.

Once you have determined the monthly amount you would like to invest, you want to make sure you invest it wisely. The strategy you choose should take into account your age, years to retirement, single or married, risk tolerance and second-life goals.

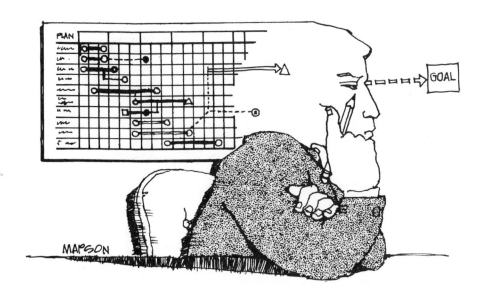

DIVERSIFY YOUR INVESTMENTS

Developing a Financial Diversification Circle is a good way in which to develop a solid financial plan. Assume, for a moment, you wish to enter your second life with assets in excess of one million dollars. You desire to accumulate this sum through a variety of investments. You are doing this because your financial comfort zone tells you to accumulate capital without taking excessive risks. In other words, you want to spread out your investments so that if one fails or drops in value, others will move up. Most financial professionals recommend diversification as a sound strategy.

Please study the model circle on the facing page. The first thing to do is decide how much capital you wish to accumulate before retirement. The circle presents five choices: $200,000, $400,000, $600,000, $800,000 or $1,000,000. Although one million may sound like an excessive amount to accumulate, keep in mind that you might have twenty years or more in which to do this. Please circle the amount you hope to achieve.

MODEL DIVERSIFICATION CIRCLE

Circle the amount of capital you hope to accumulate and do the rest of your computing as a percentage of that figure.

$200,000 $400,000 $600,000 $800,000 $1,000,000 $ _____

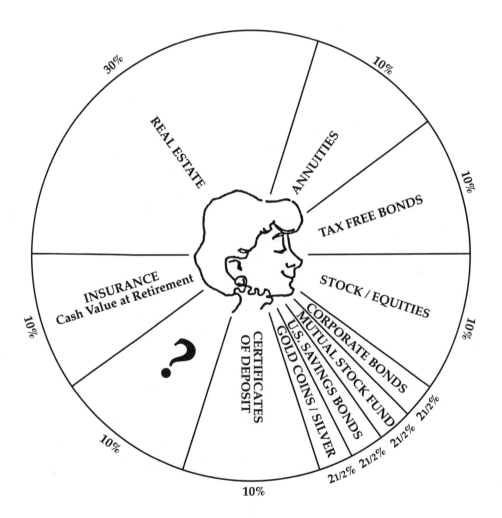

*For detailed information on the investment possibilities contained in the above circle, the reader is encouraged to discuss it with the manager of a local financial institution or financial planner.

MODEL DIVERSIFICATION CIRCLE (Continued)

EXPLANATION OF MODEL

You will notice that 30% of the total investment (represented by the model diversification circle) is in real estate. Depending upon your capital accumulation goal, this could be too large or too small and should be adjusted. It also assumes that it is your desire to have the mortgage on your home paid by the time you enter your second life.

In the model, 10% is invested in annuities, most likely via a payroll deduction. The good news with an annuity is that interest is compounded and the investment grows quickly. The bad news is that income tax will need to be paid when funds are withdrawn after retirement. To compensate for this, 10% is invested in tax-free municipal bonds. These bonds (if purchased within the state of residence) will draw interest before and after retirement and no income taxes need by paid.

Many people would invest more than 10% in high-risk stock/equities, but, in this case, the model is conservative. Corporate employees who can purchase stock in their own company at a discount usually have more funds invested in common stocks. Others prefer to be invested in mutual stock funds to further increase their diversification.

In the model, 2½% is invested in corporate bonds, treasury bills, savings bonds, and gold and silver (coins and bars) for a total of 10%. Notice, also, that 10% is invested in short-term certificates of deposit so that safety (government insured) and frequent access is possible.

Ten percent (10% also represents the cash value at the time of retirement) of insurance policies. This percentage could vary depending upon the attitude of the individual toward insurance as an investment.

Please view the model Diversification Circle as a "starter set." That is, it is a device that will help you get started but will become increasingly sophisticated as your investments grow. Once started and used as a reference point for a few years, you will discover the circle has the following advantages:

- Comparing different types of investments for balancing and diversification purposes is made easy.

- The Diversification Circle gives one a clear and easy way to interpret a bird's eye view of investments without becoming confused with traditional accounting procedures.

- Spouses who have had little or no training in accounting can communicate to each other better via the circle technique.

- Using a pencil, a Diversification Circle can be updated or adjusted frequently and easily.

- The technique is ideal for a quick review and for future planning.

- When the time comes to consider a new investment possibility, a comparison with those already in one's portfolio (circle) is facilitated.

In using the Diversification Circle approach to financial planning, it is well to keep the following in mind:

1. The model introduces only a few investment opportunities. Each should be carefully investigated and evaluated to make sure that the investment falls within the individual's financial comfort zone. New instruments (international mutual funds, commodities, etc.) should not be added until sufficient research has been made.

2. Social Security and monthly pension income should not be a part of the circle. However, income from the capital investments should be added to achieve a monthly retirement income for planning purposes. For example, at a 10% return on $400,000 (do not include real estate), annual income could be $40,000 per annum. Divided by 12 months, this means approximately $3,330 could be added to monthly income from Social Security and pension payments.

3. Although many second-lifers prefer to live from their monthly income checks plus returns from their capital investments (circle), it is obvious that some of the capital is available to spend during the various zones.

4. At a certain stage in your planning, it may be wise to take your Diversification Circle to a certified financial planner for evaluation, refinement, and expansion.

START YOUR OWN DIVERSIFICATION CIRCLE

Using the illustration below, please take time to start your personal Diversification Circle. Write in the dollar or percentage amount you hope to reach at your anticipated point of retirement. Sketch in those investments you already have and start making plans for the future.

RETIREMENT CAPITAL GOAL $_____

(Do not include income from Social Security or pensions.)

SUPPLEMENTAL PLANNING SHEET

RETIREMENT CAPITAL GOAL $ _____

TIPS FOR SUCCESSFUL INVESTING

1. Start a Diversification Circle early so that you can balance your investments according to your financial comfort zone.

2. Begin investing early so you can take advantage of compounding.

3. Always have a financial advisor so that you and your spouse are kept current on economic changes.

4. Increase your investment percentage of total income as you get closer to retirement.

5. If you should receive a lump sum pension distribution when you change jobs, don't spend it—roll it over into another tax-deferred investment.

6. Enjoy the saving and investment process. Whenever you make a change or addition to your Diversification Circle, review your plan so that your financial strategy is correlated with your second-life goals.

7. Don't be overly cautious if you're in your twenties and thirties.

8. Every now and then balance your property (home or land) investments with the rest of your portfolio. If you decide that 30% or 40% of your total assets should be in real estate, make an adjustment.

9. If you're self-employed, open a SEP-IRA or Keogh account and maintain the maximum fully tax deductible contributions (up to 13% and 20%, respectively).

10. Attend an investment seminar occasionally so that you can keep your Diversification Circle up to date with the best investments available.

TIPS ON SPENDING CAPITAL

When the matter of spending capital (savings) is introduced into a conversation, people often have mixed emotions. Should they spend some capital to enhance their own destinies or save some to enhance the lives of their children and/or grandchildren? Some people use the rule of three strategy as illustrated below.

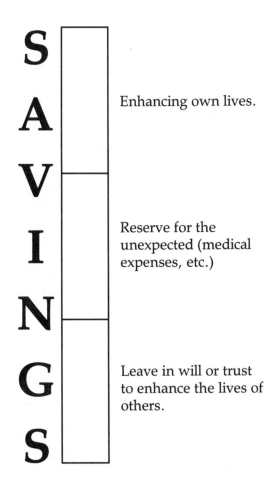

S
A
V
I
N
G
S

Enhancing own lives.

Reserve for the unexpected (medical expenses, etc.)

Leave in will or trust to enhance the lives of others.

Just what percentage is designated to each of the three divisions is, of course, up to the individual. In doing capital allocation planning of this nature, the table on the next page can be helpful.

HOW FAST WILL YOUR CAPITAL DISAPPEAR?

Some second-lifers spend only the income from their investments. They do not touch their capital. But what if you did want to dip into your nest egg? What percentage would you want to spend each year? How long would you want it to last? The table below shows how long your money would last if you spent a certain percentage each year based upon the return of the remaining capital (interest rate).

RATE OF ANNUAL WITH-DRAWAL	AVERAGE ANNUAL RATE OF RETURN ON YOUR INVESTMENT													
	1%	2%	3%	4%	5%	6%	7%	8%	9%	10%	11%	12%	13%	14%
	NUMBER OF YEARS YOUR MONEY WILL LAST													
15%	6	7	7	7	8	8	9	9	10	11	12	13	16	21
14%	7	7	8	8	8	9	10	10	11	12	14	17	22	
13%	8	8	8	9	9	10	11	12	13	15	17	23		
12%	8	9	9	10	10	11	12	14	15	18	24			
11%	9	10	10	11	12	13	14	16	19	25				
10%	10	11	12	13	14	15	17	20	26					
9%	11	12	13	14	16	18	22	28						
8%	13	14	15	17	20	23	30							
7%	15	16	18	21	25	33								
6%	18	20	23	28	36									
5%	22	25	30	41										
4%	28	35	46											
3%	40	55												
2%	69													

IDENTIFY SPENDING PRIORITIES

As difficult as it is to anticipate many years into the future, please project yourself into your second life and assume you have completed the financial goals listed in the previous pages. How would you spend your hard-earned income and perhaps some of your capital? To assist you in making such decisions, you are invited to prioritize the possibilities listed below. Do this by writing a 1 in the square opposite your top choice and so on until you have written the highest number into the last square.

PRIORITY

☐ Spending money for personal pleasures such as eating out, beauty care, dressing fashionably, etc. Do not include sports activities or traveling expenses.

☐ Entertaining friends and family.

☐ Having a special home in a special location decorated to my specifications.

☐ Traveling.

☐ Spending money on golf, tennis, and fitness programs.

☐ Having a new, fancy car.

☐ Leaving money to my children and grandchildren.

☐ Bequeathing funds to my church or other charitable organization.

☐ OTHER: _____

_____

Professional financial planners usually ask their clients to tie their financial planning to retirement goals. When you stop to think of the time gap involved, this is a most difficult challenge. Establishing such goals is necessary, however, if you are serious about enhancing your destiny.

FIVE-ZONE SPENDING STRATEGY

To give you some idea of how you might develop a second-life spending strategy, a model is presented below. This model is based upon the premise that you will want to spend your money more freely during early zones so you can reach your highest level of pleasure and fulfillment. Keep in mind, however, that some people have difficulty spending their income, let alone some of their capital.

ASSUMPTIONS

Individual starts second life at 65, lives to be 90.

Monthly income of $3,000 minimum.

Capital assets (circle) of $200,000 minimum.

Person qualifies for Medicare and maintains a strong supplemental Medi-Gap insurance program.

AGE 65	AGE 77	AGE 85	AGE 89	AGE 90
TRANSITION ZONE	**SERENDIPITY ZONE**	**SWEET ZONE**	**REFLECTIVE ZONE**	**SUNSET ZONE**
2 Years	10 Years	8 Years	4 Years	1 Year
Allocate $5,000 to be spent on special vacation to launch second life and help with adjustment. Through planning, spend all income. If necessary, make special purchases or take short trips.	Spend all income as in Phase I. Before 10 years are over, reduce original capital by 25% to reach fulfillment goals.	Continue to spend income. Reduce capital by another 25% for frequent but less ambitious fulfillments.	Spend income. Start process of giving to others.	Take care of final expenses and continue the distribution of funds to family or friends.

REVIEW

Tentative answers to the questions on this page are necessary to give your financial plan substance. Use a pencil so that you can make changes later. Please keep in mind that these are *planning figures.* Calculated guesses are encouraged.

1. Enter (once again) your anticipated age upon retirement.

2. Keeping in mind (as we all must do) that health is the big joker in our lives, enter the number of years you anticipate you will have available for your second life. Base your answer upon:

> Your age when you plan to retire
> Heredity factors (age of father & mother)
> State of health at present time
> Health program for the future
> Attitude toward your aging process
> Life expectancy table (see page 7)

3. Enter the amount of monthly income you expect after retirement. Include Social Security, company and/or military pensions. Do not include annuities.

4. Enter the retirement capital goal (Diversification Circle) you hope to take with you into your second life.

5. Enter the amount of monthly income you believe your Diversification Circle will produce once you retire. (A rough estimate based upon current interest rates will suffice—7% of total figure may be close).

6. Add the figures you produced in 3 and 5 above and enter in the square provided. This is your anticipated monthly income figure.

Whether the figures above are for one person or the combined income of two people, factor in the increase in salary or salaries anticipated between now and future retirement date.

BOOK II

PART 2

ACTIVITY
PLANNING

SELECTING
YOUR ACTIVITY
PREFERENCES

Activity choices are the key to pleasure and fulfillment at any time of life. Field testing of an early second-life planning guide produced the data in the box below. Twenty participants (about to retire) were asked to check, from a list of more than 50 activities, the top 10 they would prefer in the three middle zones.

ACTIVITY PREFERENCES IN THE THREE PRIMARY ZONES

SEREDIPITY ZONE	SWEET ZONE	SPIRITUAL ZONE
1. Travel	1. Travel	1. Family activities
2. Social activities	2. Outdoor walks	2. Outdoor walks
3. Reading	3. Hobbies	3. Home activities
4. Part-time work	4. Reading	4. Television
5. Family activities	5. Home activities	5. Time alone
6. Outdoor walks	6. Educational classes	6. Hobbies
7. Volunteer work	7. Family activities	7. Reading
8. Hobbies	8. Exercise programs	8. Private talks
9. Exercise programs	9. Cultural activities	9. Social activities
10. Religious activities	10. Card games	10. Religious activities

---

The above replies indicate the following:

• Travel is the most popular of all activities.

• Reading was second in popularity among those surveyed.

• Hobbies are most appreciated in the Sweet Zone.

• Outdoor walks are a popular activity among all zones.

• Television was not listed in the top 10 preferred activities until the Spiritual Zone (this does not indicate how much time was spent watching television).

THE ABOVE PREFERENCES INDICATE ACTIVITIES OTHER PEOPLE PREFER—*NOT* WHAT YOU MAY DESIRE. WITH THIS IN MIND, COMPLETE THE EXERCISE ON THE FOLLOWING PAGE.

"YOU TRY IT!"

ACTIVITY PREFERENCES IN THE THREE PRIMARY ZONES

SERENDIPITY ZONE	SWEET ZONE	SPIRITUAL ZONE
1. _____	1. _____	1. _____
2. _____	2. _____	2. _____
3. _____	3. _____	3. _____
4. _____	4. _____	4. _____
5. _____	5. _____	5. _____
6. _____	6. _____	6. _____
7. _____	7. _____	7. _____
8. _____	8. _____	8. _____
9. _____	9. _____	9. _____
10. _____	10. _____	10. _____

START AN IDEA FILE FOR SERENDIPITY ZONE

Some people think it a good idea for those in their thirties and forties to start an *Idea File* for the Serendipity Zone. If this appeals to you, here are some ideas to get you started.

1. If you can qualify and a course is available near you, enroll in a beginning gerontology class to learn more about the aging process.

2. Spend some time with a few people who are making the most of their second life. Ask questions like: "What can I do now to prepare for a better retirement?" Having a good second-life model is a good idea!

3. Try to take your vacations to check out what might be the best living environment for you in your second life.

4. Review your financial plan more frequently.

5. Explore the idea of having a Plan A, B, and C as defined below:

> PLAN A—your present career.
>
> PLAN B—preparations for a second career should your first one disappear or you become disenchanted with it.
>
> PLAN C—investigating and preparing for a second-life part-time career.

6. _____

7. _____

8. _____

9. _____

10. _____

> USING THE ABOVE AS A MODEL, START AN IDEA FILE ON THE SERENDIPITY, SWEET AND SPIRITUAL ZONES. USE THE NEXT THREE PAGES.

SERENDIPITY ZONE IDEA FILE (follow the model on page 104)

SWEET ZONE IDEA FILE (follow the model on page 104)

SPIRITUAL ZONE IDEA FILE (follow the model on page 104)

DO A SERENDIPITY SCENARIO

Assume you are taking a seminar on retirement planning, and your leader has divided the class into small groups of five individuals. Each member of each group is requested to take five minutes and outline a story (scenario) that might constitute the essence of his time in the Serendipity Zone. You have been told that you will be asked to use this outline to give a verbal report within the small group; if yours is the most romantic and exciting the leader will choose you to give the report to the class as a whole.

Write out your scenario outline below:

_____

_____

_____

_____

_____

_____

_____

_____

_____

_____

_____

_____

_____

_____

_____

What chance do you give yourself of fulfilling your serendipity secenario?

Less than 50% ☐   More than 50% ☐

VERIFY
YOUR ATTITUDE
TOWARD A
SECOND LIFE

You have no doubt convinced yourself by now that your attitude toward a fulfilling second life for yourself is the key to whether you make it happen. Your conviction is justified!

Admittedly, this book (and guide) is designed to give the reader a positive attitude toward a second life. It is the underlying theme. Now, you may say to yourself, isn't this creating a positive illusion? The answer is yes, but it is necessary to do so. In short, the idea is to create a dream scenario of a second life in the mind of the reader even if the reality (when it arrives) does not live up to the dream. The rationale behind this is simple. A mind that dwells excessively on reality is not always a healthy mind because reality can be mostly negative. Answer? Concentrate on the positive factors and diminish the negative. *This will give you a more fulfilling second life.*

So how do you *really* feel about a second life? Are you sufficiently positive to enhance your destiny? The following exercise will help you find out.

SECOND-LIFE ATTITUDE SCALE

This exercise is designed to help people measure their attitudes toward a second life. It is usually enjoyable for two or more people seriously interested in their future to do the exercise separately and then match and discuss results. Please read statements at both ends of the scale and then circle the number that best reflects how you honestly feel. If you circle a 10, your attitude could not be more positive. If you circle a 1, your attitude could not be more negative. Most people rate themselves somewhere between the two extremes. You will be able to score and evaluate your responses at the end of the exercise.

I accept the second-life challenge with high enthusiasm.	10 9 8 7 6 5 4 3 2 1	I'll coast along and see what happens.
I plan to make my second life more exciting than my first.	10 9 8 7 6 5 4 3 2 1	When I get there I just want to rest and relax.
I already view each zone as a separate opportunity.	10 9 8 7 6 5 4 3 2 1	My attitude is negative toward the phase idea.
I like my odds for living a long life.	10 9 8 7 6 5 4 3 2 1	Who cares about longevity?
I'm going to be a late-bloomer.	10 9 8 7 6 5 4 3 2 1	I'm going to be a non-bloomer.
The more positive I am about my second-life the better my life will be now.	10 9 8 7 6 5 4 3 2 1	One life has no influence upon the other.
Fulfillment opportunities abound in one's second life.	10 9 8 7 6 5 4 3 2 1	I only want to fill a rocking chair.
The prospects of a second life deserve advance planning.	10 9 8 7 6 5 4 3 2 1	Planning leads to disappointment.
I want to experience the best of all five zones.	10 9 8 7 6 5 4 3 2 1	The Serendipity Zone is the only one of interest to me.
I love the second life idea from start to finish.	10 9 8 7 6 5 4 3 2 1	Retirement is still just retirement.

TOTAL [   ]

If you rated yourself 80 or above, your attitude is highly positive; chances are good you will make the most out of your second life. Give it your best! If you rated yourself between 50 and 80, you still have reservations about a second life. If you rated yourself under 50, please rate yourself again at a later date.

BOOK II
PART 3

ZONE BY ZONE
PLANNING

TRANSITION ZONE

Questions on this page discuss exclusively the first year or two of your second life.

1. Most people start their second life with a vacation or so-called "honeymoon" period so they can free themselves from the responsibilities and hang-ups of their first life. Some take cruises, others go on extended RV trips, still others go to their favorite resort, visit friends and relatives, or take many short trips.

   Do you plan a "honeymoon" period?   YES ☐   NO ☐

   For how long?   _____

   Where will you go?   _____

   Based upon what you learned about the difficulty in making a transition (chapter 9), how long do you think it will take you to make your passage? Include time spent on honeymoon.

   ☐

2. Once a transition vacation is over, most people get around to revising and implementing their plans. Check those factors that you anticipate will be most important to you when the time comes.

   ☐ Finding a fulfilling part-time job.

   ☐ Finding a satisfying volunteer involvement.

   ☐ Learning to live a life of pure leisure without boredom.

3. Do you intend to spend all of your income during the Transition Zone? This would include Social Security, pensions, and income from investments included in your Diversification Circle.

   YES ☐   NO ☐

4. Do you intend to set aside some money ahead of time for your transition honeymoon? If so, what amount?

   $ ☐

SERENDIPITY ZONE

Most people anticipate an average of 13 years in this zone. Many feel the hours, days, and years are their most precious to be found in either life. Please start your planning for the Serendipity Zone by answering these questions.

1. From the activity preferences (pages 102 and 103), select the *five* primary ones you wish to pursue in the Serendipity Zone. *Please feel free to add one or more activities not found on the list.*

    1. _____

    2. _____

    3. _____

    4. _____

    5. _____

Other:

    6. _____

    7. _____

2. Do you feel you need a challenge, mission, or goal over and above what you listed? Perhaps something for which you are still searching?

YES ☐   NO ☐

3. Health permitting, how many years do you hope to spend in the Serendipity Zone? [   ]

                                    Years

4. List below where you hope to reside during this zone of your second life. Do you desire to live in the mountains, near the beach, adjacent to a golf course, foreign country, or where you live now? Please list the type of residence and the facilities you expect (free-standing home, condo, mobile home park, etc.).

_____

_____

_____

5. Are you planning to spend all of your monthly retirement income (including interest on investments) during this period? YES ☐   NO ☐

6. Will you be willing to diminish your capital during this period of high activity and possibly travel? YES ☐   NO ☐

7. If your answer was YES, what percentage?

10%   25%   50%   75%   Other?_____

SWEET ZONE

People enter this zone at different times but usually between the ages of 70 and 80. Those in natural, good health often spend 10 years in the Sweet Zone. Many view it as a positive challenge that can provide many rewards and fulfillments not previously experienced.

1. What is your attitude toward the Sweet Zone? Can you be happier and more content in a less active lifestyle? Please place a ☑ in front of those statements below you feel positive about.

   ☐ I am enthusiastic about developing a plan that will make the Sweet Zone more pleasurable than the Serendipity Zone.

   ☐ I hope to be happier in this zone than all others.

   ☐ The promise of less activity and more fulfillment through the right balance intrigues me.

2. From the list (on pages 102 and 103) select the five activities you wish to save and pursue in the Sweet Zone. *Please try to add one or two activities (goals, missions) not found on the list.*

   1. _____
   2. _____
   3. _____
   4. _____
   5. _____
   Other:
   6. _____
   7. _____

3. Is there one outstanding project or dream you wish to continue from the Serendipity into the Sweet Zone? If so, list below.

   _____

4. How many years would you like to spend in the Sweet Zone? ☐ Years

5. What percentage of your *remaining* capital might you be willing to spend in this zone? ☐ %

SPIRITUAL ZONE

Most people who reach this zone are happy and content to spend more time at home. This does not mean, however, that some social events and important activities are out of reach. Their world may become smaller, but favorite involvements are still enjoyed.

1. Assuming you may reach this advanced zone, how might you plan for it? What happens will depend primarily upon your attitude at the time. Please ☑ the statements below that you hope will reflect your attitude.

   ☐ I want to make it to the Spiritual Zone and make the most of it when I get there.

   ☐ I want to become a Master Senior (one who can look back knowing the previous zones have been successful) and be a model for those who are younger.

   ☐ As far as possible, I want to remain active.

2. Please write out the five activities you hope to participate in during this period.

   1. _____
   2. _____
   3. _____
   4. _____
   5. _____

3. Would you like to add any of the following to your list? If so, place a check in the appropriate squares.

   ☐ Writing memoirs.

   ☐ Distributing possessions among family/friends.

   ☐ Reminiscing with family and friends who care enough about you to listen.

4. Knowing how much time you plan to spend in previous zones, how many years would you like to have in the Spiritual Zone? ☐☐☐

   Years

5. Knowing how much of your capital you have planned to spend in previous zones, how much of that which remains would you like to spend in this zone?

   ☐ All of it.

   ☐ Half of it.

   ☐ Only a small part of what is left.

SUNSET ZONE

Many people, due to health problems, are forced to speed through one or more of the first four zones. Assume, however, you have a long and involving second life and wind up at the doorstep of the Sunset Zone with enough time for a few activities. Which three from the list below would be most important to you?

☐ Seeking spiritual fulfillment by reading religious literature.

☐ Putting relationships in order.

☐ Having a final fling or two.

☐ Taking a trip back to your roots.

☐ Setting up a few family gatherings.

☐ Having fun disposing of personal possessions.

☐ Making peace with yourself.

☐ Attending church services.

☐ Discussing your two lives with those you love.

OTHER: _____

_____

1. Do you feel those who reach fulfillment in earlier zones will be more apt to accept the Sunset Zone with greater inner strength?

YES ☐   NO ☐

2. Do you feel that by accepting the Sunset Zone years ahead of time that earlier years are enhanced?

YES ☐   NO ☐

REVIEW OF ZONE PLANNING

It is natural and advisable to give the Serendipity Zone top priority as far as planning is concerned. This does not mean, however, that you should neglect your planning in the other four zones. Here is a priority list of the five zones that indicates the most significant benefits to be derived from each one. The benefit listed for one zone can not be fully duplicated in another.

SERENDIPITY ZONE: Top priority because it is in this zone that you will have more time, energy, and money to spend.

SWEET ZONE: Second priority because there is less pressure to succeed, a more balanced comfort zone can be reached, and the zone can last for many years.

TRANSITION ZONE: Although short in time, it is during this period that one makes the adjustment for an entire second life.

SPIRITUAL ZONE: Personal growth is more limited to mental activities.

SUNSET ZONE: Short in time. Only spiritual fulfillment a possibility.

Unfinished business needs to be completed.

BOOK II

PART 4
COMMITMENT
SUMMARY

If you are to enhance your destiny to the fullest possible extent, three factors must be present.

1. Expectations for a positive future must be high. Those who have the courage to plan an upbeat second life will benefit significantly in comparison to those who do not.

2. Sound financial planning (starting early) is essential in order to create the kind of second life you desire when you get there. You pay the price for a second life whether you do the planning or not.

3. To make the most of a second life you (along with everyone else) need a mission, purpose, or energizing goal. A challenge is necessary to keep you away from trivialization which can turn your second life into a dull retirement.

Attitudinal Changes

    Barriers to Fulfillment

        Commitments I Intend to Keep

ATTITUDINAL CHANGES

You will recall that on page 79 you answered the same questions listed below. Please answer the questions a second time and match with your previous answers to see if there have been any changes in your attitude.

QUESTIONS

1. Is 30 too young to explore the possibilities of a second life?

    Yes ☐ No ☐

2. What year do you intend to start your second life?

    Year _____

3. What age would you like to achieve in your second life?

    Age _____

4. Are you negative about your years after 60?

    Yes ☐ No ☐ Undecided ☐

5. Do you accept the premise that a strategy is necessary to make the most out of your second life?

    Yes ☐ No ☐ Undecided ☐

6. Has the term "second life" started to replace the R word in your vocabulary?

    Yes ☐ No ☐

7. Do you feel your second life prospects are good enough to start improving your health now?

    Yes ☐ No ☐ Undecided ☐

8. Are you denying yourself too much now in order to build a big nest egg later?

    Yes ☐ No ☐ Undecided ☐

9. Do you intend to make the attitude connection? That is, develop a strategy good enough to improve your present attitude?

    Yes ☐ No ☐ Undecided ☐

10. Will you need a part-time job or substantial volunteer involvement in your second life?

    Yes ☐ No ☐ Undecided ☐

BARRIERS TO FULFILLMENT

Whether 30, 50, or 70, this exercise will help you pinpoint roadblocks that may keep you from reaching the kind of serendipitous (lighthearted) living that you desire. Please read the complete list and then ☑ the three barriers that you feel are most apt to keep you from reaching your personal goals in this zone.

☐ Too much worry over personal health.

☐ Failure to take the initiative to discover and participate in new adventures.

☐ Being held back by a spouse or other person whom you love and respect.

☐ Consistent doubts about your own creativity.

☐ Fearful of taking risks.

☐ Tunnel vision that keeps you from seeing the true possibilities of the Serendipity Zone.

☐ Inability to maintain a positive attitude.

☐ Refusing to set goals.

☐ Too lazy.

☐ Allowing other people to inundate you with their problems so that you do not reach your own pleasure potential.

☐ Refusing to spend money for your own personal happiness—even though you have it to spend.

☐ Unwillingness to explore spiritual fulfillments.

☐ OTHER:

_____

_____

COMMITMENTS I INTEND TO KEEP

(Check those commitments listed below
you intend to honor.)

- ☐ I intend to talk more about a "second life"
  and, when possible, eliminate the use
  of the R word.

- ☐ Now that I have a start on a second-life strategy, I intend to make
  improvements in my first life.

- ☐ I am going to discuss the zone idea with others.

- ☐ I am going to rethink my first-life savings and investment goals and
  gear them more in the direction of my second-life plans.

- ☐ Starting immediately, I am going to initiate and maintain an
  improved diet and exercise plan.

- ☐ I intend to develop more fulfilling leisure activities now so I will be
  better prepared for my second life. If this means taking lessons
  (bridge?), returning to school (photography class?), or involving
  myself in a group activity, I will do so.

- ☐ I intend to develop a Plan B as a replacement for my present career
  (Plan A). In doing this, I will give special attention to one that I can
  take into my second life on a part-time basis.

- ☐ I intend to introduce and discuss the zone concept with my parents
  and grandparents so I can verify some of my thoughts and improve
  relationships with them.

- ☐ I intend to enroll in a retirement planning seminar when one is
  available.

- ☐ I expect to periodically review and update this plan so it will
  continue to help my positive attitude.

BOOK III

WHAT YOUR SECOND LIFE MIGHT BE LIKE

> *"IF YOU FEAR*
>
> *THE FUTURE*
>
> *YOU MAY*
>
> *DISQUALIFY*
>
> *YOURSELF FOR*
>
> *THE PRESENT."*
>
> E.N. Chapman

Chapter 1
HONEYMOON TIME

> *"I'm sixty-five and I guess that puts me in with the geriatrics but if there were fifteen months in every year, I'd only be forty eight."*
> James Thurber

Ahhh—throwing off the frustrations of work, adjusting to greater freedom, and making the passage to a new, refreshing way of life! At the beginning it is bon voyage and honeymoon time, but adjustments may be necessary later.

A minimum of one year is required for a person to make a safe passage into a fulfilling second life. Sometimes it takes three or four years, and a few never make it at all. This happens when the individual keeps looking back and winds up in limbo, often returning to full-time work.

Once into the transition zone, reality sets in and questions surface. Am I ready to deal with all of this new and unexpected freedom? What am I going to do with all of the extra time? How do I reorganize myself to avoid down periods? Should I go back to work?

> Carol had been an executive assistant to a vice president of a large firm located in a modern, elegant headquarters. Her position carried status and gave her the opportunity to have friends in high places. It was her style to make a fashion statement each morning when she arrived for work. When her position was eliminated, Carol (55) took a look at the financial side of her retirement plan and decided to start her second life early. First she took a "honeymoon" cruise to the south seas. Second, she started making improvements around the home. Third, she started to fall apart psychologically.

> How could this happen? Without knowing it, she was going through a passage to find a second-life identity to replace the work-oriented one she had left behind. Carol needed to be someone important again.

HONEYMOON TIME (Continued)

Eventually she made the transition by converting her love of travel and clerical skills into a temporary part-time assignment with a small travel agency. Carol, like many others, found it necessary to make a major adjustment in her plan. It wasn't easy.

Not everyone needs a part-time job as a bridge to a successful second-life job. But almost everyone encounters a few bumps or stormy periods in making the transition. Like taking a voyage, the smoother the trip, the more shipboard activities can be enjoyed, but even the captain cannot guarantee a perfect passage.

Although a few people seem to make quick transitions into their second lives, more advance planning is needed by most. How much money should be set aside for a honeymoon? Will a part-time involvement be required? Should I plan two or three years for this zone? A good attitude is to expect the best, but not to rush the transition process. Your entire second life will be based upon the quality of the adjustment made.

BEHAVIORAL CHARACTERISTICS

Here are some behavioral patterns people often exhibit as they reject or pass through the transition zone.

- Exuberance the first few months, with possible moodiness and depression when the honeymoon is over.

- Some find themselves doing crazy things they would have viewed dimly before retirement.

- Disenchantment over plans. "Why didn't somebody tell me this is the way it would be?"

- Feeling great over financial planning when income turns out to be as good or better than expected.

- Feeling lost over what to do with so much free time.

- Adjusting to an unnecessary concern over a minor health problem or major expense not anticipated.

- Realignment and reevaluation of human relationships. Missing those still working; finding new friends.

A yo-yo behavioral pattern similar to that described above is natural and simply means the individual is finding it necessary to adjust and fine-tune an original plan. At this point, many will reconsider using the zones as a blueprint around which they can design better strategies. Others will recognize the value of using the zones for financial planning. Still others will start to use them as a timing guide to spread out their second life so that steady and continuous fulfillment is possible. Those who decide to use the five zones as a compass to guide them through their second lives will speed up their transition and discover they have more confidence in the future.

THREE TYPICAL LIFESTYLES

There are as many paths to a successful second life as there are people who make the journey. No "right" or "model" blueprint exists, but some designs can be more closely synchronized with the five zones than others. Consider the following.

The Disengagers.   These inner-directed people decide to live out their second lives far away from the mainstream. They disengage themselves early by moving to an isolated area so their desire for detachment is communicated to family and friends. Fulfillment is found in a more contemplative, withdrawn, low-activity mode with only an occasional entry into a social environment.

> Jane and Brad devoted their first lives to achieving financial and social success. Upon retirement they made a big swing in the other direction where they would deal with only a few relationships and other pressures. A major part of their plan was having a home in a mountain area where a secluded, pristine life was possible.

Disengagers may opt for fewer people contacts and less urban congestion, but the five zones can be as important to their planning as to others. For example, you only need a few human contacts and a few trips to make the most of a Serendipity Zone. Many who isolate themselves too far, however, decide to return to the mainstream more frequently than they anticipated.

HONEYMOON TIME (Continued)

The Concentrators.   These enthusiastic individuals zero in and build their second lives around a single activity, mission or involvement. Their plan is not a blueprint, but a single goal. Some try to convert a shallow hobby into a second life work. Others become volunteers. Some live out their first lives again by raising grandchildren. Most of these people do not seek a balanced blend of leisure activities, fulfillment endeavors, and social involvements.

> Alice was a hard-working government employee for 30 years. In her second life she turned her focus on her family and garden, turning down opportunities to travel and other pleasure opportunities. Although her family and few friends thought her life narrow and boring, she claimed it was what she wanted and was happy and fulfilled.

If introduced to the five zones, concentrators would probably consider them foreign to their needs and refuse to give them consideration.

The Replacers.   These fortunate individuals have a capacity to accept their losses and quickly replace them with other activites.

> When Richard and Gena could no longer do repair work on their RV, they sold it and moved into a mobile park near a golf course; when they tired of golf, they moved into a center there they could do crafts with others; when they tired of crafts, they started taking cruises. As soon as Richard and Gena became interested in one activity, they started looking for a replacement.

Nomadic by nature, replacers have a good attitude as far as making the most out of their second lives. The problem is they act on impulse without the advantage of a master plan. As a result, they often accept replacements too soon and thus fail to make the most of the five zones. Instead of placing activities within the best zone, they rush through a series of activities prematurely. Once they have run through their inadequate list they throw up their hands and turn to television full-time. Most replacers could double their pleasure if they accepted and applied the zone concept.

UPDATING A BLUEPRINT

Unfortunately, disengagers, concentrators, and replacers all have two things in common: (1) They enter their second life with a weak plan or none at all; (2) They fail to use the transition period to replace a negative mental set with a positive view of what lies ahead. As a result, they fail to live up to the potential their second lives offer. To avoid these mistakes, you may wish to consider these suggestions.

- Take time during the transition zone to evaluate, revise, and fine tune your master blueprint.

- Become more acquainted with future zones so you know what to do now and what you should save until later.

- Leave all excess baggage from your previous work lifestyle behind.

- Accept the challenge of your second life on a zone-by-zone basis.

- Recognize you have a better future than you thought.

Chapter 2
KICKING UP YOUR HEELS

> *"I'll never make the mistake of being seventy again."*
> Casey Stengel

Do you want to become involved in something creative, adventuresome, or unusual in your second life? If so, plan for them in this zone. This period should be full of fun, excitement, achievement, and risk-taking. Your battle cry should be "Let's do it now."

Serendipity was selected as the title for this, the longest and most active zone, for the following reasons.

- Serendipity signals a release from responsibilities and opens the mind to a more light-hearted approach to living.

- The word also signals a time to travel to new geographical locations and to direct the mind into new levels of thought and creativity.

- The third message transmitted is that with a serendipitous attitude, unforeseen "good things" can happen to you.

The word serendipity was coined by Horace Walpole in 1754 when he put the fairy-tale *The Three Princes of Serendip* to paper. It is a delightful story of three princes who travel from kingdom to kingdom in a lighthearted, compassionate manner. In helping others solve their problems, they enhance their own lives.

Serendipity is a carefree, "happiness" word. Behind the expression is a fascinating concept that can lift one above the mundane. The magic occurs when we realize a lighter approach can cause some good things to happen in our lives.

I believe there is what might be called a serendipitous *attitude*, a kind of mental set that helps us view our environment in a more humorous and forgiving manner. This attitude is within the reach of everyone; and, when achieved, fortuitous things happen. For example, when you have a lighthearted, mischievous, festive way of looking at things, others are intrigued and invite you to share beautiful experiences with them. A serendipitous attitude is catching!

KICKING UP YOUR HEELS (Continued)

It is important to believe in serendipity at any stage of life (the earlier the better), but it has greater significance after an individual has made his or her transition into a second life. If takes away some of the negative feeling that can go with wrinkles, slowness, and pill-taking. Serendipity, and all it stands for, makes aging easier. No one should attempt a second life without it.

Serendipitous pursuits fall into such categories as traveling, consulting, doing part-time work (for money or as a volunteer) that contributes to the lives of others, starting a very small hobby-type business that takes no more than 20 hours per week, and a host of pleasure activities. The choices are endless, exciting, and challenging, and everone can qualify. All it takes is the desire to be a participant in life instead of an observer.

OPPORTUNITY TO CUT LOOSE

Under concepts encouraged by previous generations, post-work years were to be quiet and golden. Today, the "mellow" days are postponed until the Spiritual Zone. Early years are full of action, involvement, and accomplishment. Due to good planning and medical advancements, some people are successful in stretching the Serendipity Zone for 20 years or more.

Time spent within this exciting zone should be devoted to doing what you have always really wanted to do. It is a time of self-actualization. Like spring wild flowers, "late bloomers" surface and prosper.

> Delores and Hugo, both certified public accountants, started their financial planning early and had designed an enviable plan. Once their transition zone was over (they took a two-week "honeymoon" trip to Hawaii and caught up on a long list of home improvements), Delores and Hugo launched into their big adventure of seeing America. They did this by purchasing a senior airline pass permitting them to fly to any destination within the system for a single, annual purchase price. For the first three years, they were traveling almost half the time. Using discounts for motels, car rentals, and restaurants, the pair

visited over 30 states and lived it up all the way! So much so that toward the end they were showing signs of burnout. Then, with their big second-life goal satisfied, they settled back to a less demanding pace, determined to use their serendipitous attitude to satisfy as many remaining active goals on their list as possible.

Like Delores and Hugo, most people sense that this zone gives them their big chance to cut loose. Because it is the period when dreams are fulfilled or lost, the Serendipity Zone requires more advance planning than others. The opportunities can never again be duplicated because you have almost everything you had in your first life, without having to work to pay for it. Some people like to call it the "now or never" zone. Consider these benefits.

Unlimited freedom.   The world is your oyster. You are free to do what you want as long as your ventures are legal. No boss! No work schedule! And your energy levels remain high. Under this new environment, your creative juices can spring to the surface. You can actually undertake some of the adventures you have dreamed about for years.

Fun without guilt.   Some people have the work ethic so imbedded into their psyche they have trouble with the Serendipity Zone. They feel they must accomplish something each day to enjoy the hours that remain. This attitude is okay up to a point, but hopefully when the time comes you will feel that you have made your major contribution to society and can live it up without the "guilts." (What a feeling!)

Money-spending time.   Remember the money tree? Spending money during the Serendipity Zone may bring twice as much enjoyment as later. We are talking about inflationary possibilities as well as having energy to enjoy the activity selected. (Are you planning to spend your income as well as some capital?)

STRETCHING YOUR SERENDIPITY TIME

Most people, understandably, want to make their Serendipity Zone last as long as possible. And why not? Sometimes, however, adjustments are necessary. Here are two examples.

> *The Younger Wife.* It didn't take Janice long to sense that her husband's surgery would cause a midcourse correction and trip him into the Sweet one ahead of time. How did she handle the situation? She initiated a series of conversations about adjusting their original plan. Her approach was to recognize the rewards of both the Serendipity and Sweet Zones. Janice proposed that she stay part of the time in the Serendipity Zone and part with her husband in the Sweet Zone. "You want to stay home working on investments and hobbies. I want to be out in the community. We give each other some space during the day. At night, and when on trips, we can enjoy activities together. Eventually I will join you full time in your comfort zone. Until then, we have made an adjustment best for both of us."

How did the adjustment work out? Beautifully! Both Janice and her husband were able to enjoy the rewards available in both comfort zones.

> *The Slow Reversal.* When it took Florence six months to recover from her accident she became so discouraged that she wanted to move into the next zone immediately. Sensing her attitude, Helen, a close friend and golfing partner, made this comment: "Florence, it would be easy for you to give up and slip into the old rocking chair syndrome, but it wouldn't be fair to you or your husband. You demonstrated today that you can play nine holes of golf. In a few weeks you'll be back up to 18. Keep trying. You are coming back faster than you think."

How did it work out? With the help of her friends and husband, Florence had eight more highly active years in the Serendipity Zone.

No one can prescribe the way you should make the most of the Serendipity Zone. However, when you get there, don't ignore those promises and plans you made when you were 40 or younger. Fulfill them!

BEHAVIORAL CHARACTERISTICS

What are a few typical patterns you might discover among those in this zone? How do they differ from characteristics of the same people going through their transition? You can observe many of them engaged in the following:

- Initiating new exercise and diet programs
- Demonstrating a higher level of personal confidence
- Spending more time (and money) in clothing and beauty shops
- Traveling, traveling, traveling
- Making more decisive decisions
- Speaking up more freely
- Demonstrating adventuresome attitudes
- Laughing more

To further develop your understanding of the Serendipity Zone, study these cases.

The Lawyer From Oshkosh.   I met a lawyer from Wisconsin who had designed a unique serendipity lifestyle. He lost his wife 10 years previously, and, after taking a sabbatical for a few years, returned to a limited law practice (six months work/six months leisure) which permitted frequent vacation trips to different parts of the world. He made this comment: ''The only thing that would cause me to change my lifestyle would be a serious medical problem.''

The Deliberate Skip.   Herb and Rachel devoted 41 years to the operation of their hightly successful retail store. They averaged almost 12 hours of work per day and took few vacations. But all of this time they had a plan to sell out at the appropriate time and move into a new life where they could relax and enjoy their hard-earned money. When they first heard about the five zones, they made a decision to skip the high-activity Serendipity Zone and move directly into the Sweet Zone.

Did it work? It was a good solution for two years, but when their level of energy returned, they were anxious to have some high-energy activities and soon returned to the Serendipity Zone.

The Sudden Transition. Velma's friends and family members were surprised when she resigned her part-time job and announced she was slowing down. She explained her decision to her best friend Jessica: "When I lost Jake 10 years ago, the part-time job was perfect. The involvement was more important than the money, and I still had time for trips and vacations. But the job kept demanding more of my time and energy. I was almost working full time. So I decided to gain more time for myself. I no longer want organizational involvements. I guess you could call it a case of people "burnout."

How did it work out for Velma? She made a successful move into the Sweet Zone and finds it most rewarding. Her advice to others: "When the time is right, don't be afraid to find your own comfort zone. Nobody will find it for you."

SERENDIPITY ZONE SUGGESTIONS

How long should one stay in zone two? Given reasonably good health, it is usually best to remain as long as the effort it takes will not subtract from the joys available in future zones. Only by knowing yourself and coming to terms with your individual aging process can you recognize when you have outgrown one zone and, for greater pleasure and fulfillment, should make the transition to the next zone. Only by knowing the opportunities and limitations of all five zones can one make the best decision.

In planning for your serendipity years, consider the following:

- Become wrapped up in a zone-two project of your choice but not to the point you neglect your health. There's a lot of good living ahead.

- Zone two is the ideal time to go back to school. Elder Hostel programs present many serendipitous opportunities.

- It could be a mistake to decide how much time you wish to spend in this zone until you know more about what future zones offer.

- Keep in mind that if you become a second-life workaholic (40 or 50 hours per week) you return to life one. You can't have the advantages of both lives at the same time.

- Not spending money while you are in the Serendipity Zone can be regretted later.

Chapter 3
LIGHTEN UP, MABLE

> *"I'm saving that rocker for the day*
> *when I feel as old as I really am."*
> Dwight D. Eisenhower

Sooner or later there comes a time for a slower pace—a time to shed some of the challenges you wanted in the Serendipity Zone. It is learning to say no to certain invitations so you can save energy for other, more rewarding activities. Staying home with simple pleasures becomes more enjoyable than accepting strenuous outside involvements. Some of this occurs because of lower energy levels; some by preference.

Golfers talk about the "sweet spot" on their clubs. When a nine iron hits the ball in the sweet spot (center), it will travel straighter and farther. Professional tennis players often refer to the "sweet spot" on their tennis rackets. There is also a sweet spot or zone in retirement.

- It is a zone in perfect balance between outside activities (traveling, dancing, socializing) and inside activities (reading, woodworking, enjoying television).

- Like the serendipity zone, finding it and making it work requires a positive attitude. You must believe you have a Sweet Zone of your own and accept the challenge of finding it.

- The phrase "Home Sweet Home" comes into play because it is during this period that home pleasures become more important to most people.

SEEKING THE RIGHT BALANCE

Of all five stages, the Sweet Zone is the most illusive. Because of this, people seem to divide themselves into three groups.

(1) Some people never find a comfortable, rewarding Sweet Zone of their own. You know this happens because you enjoy these people while they are still in the Serendipity Zone and then, a year or so later, you discover they have become reclusive. You get the impression that these individuals have passed through the Sweet Zone without knowing it was there. Did they miss it because they were unable to find a middle ground between the Serendipity and Spiritual Zones?

SEEKING THE RIGHT BALANCE

(2) A second group of people seems to find their individual Sweet Zone but, for some reason, they can't hang on to it for long. They hit the jackpot, but within a year or two the balance that made it possible slips away. Do these people find the pull toward security and their television sets too strong to resist?

(3) The third group is composed of those who find a good balance and, knowing the value of what they have, hang on with determination and skill. Some appear to remain within their Sweet Zones for eight, 10, or 15 years. Once they achieve this comfort zone, they are so happy they monitor their balance carefully. You hear them talking about the "right tempo," and the "proper pace." With discipline and control they refuse to give up a select number of activities (traveling, church involvements, social events, etc.) and they also refuse to become "couch potatoes."Instead of watching television excessively, they devote their home time to hobbies, creative prusuits, and entertaining others. Their attitude is, "Why shouldn't I have the best of both worlds?"

Interviews indicated that some individuals prefer and are happier in the Sweet than the Serendipity Zone. They claim they gain more pleasure and fulfillment. A few go so far as to say that the Sweet Zone is the jewel in the second-life crown. A number of individuals told me that they should have entered the zone sooner.

TIPS ON ACHIEVING GOOD BALANCE

How have enthusiastic individuals achieved their success in the Sweet Zone? How did they reach the right balance? Interviews point to these possibilities:

- Through good time management based upon a new set of priorities, they turned off low-rewarding activities and retained high-rewarding ones to add to a new list of home-oriented pleasures.

- They had the courage to close out a few human relationships that were no longer mutually rewarding.

- Through experimentation and patience, they achieved a satisfactory blend between home and special outside activities.

- They took two or more vacations each year to avoid getting into "ruts" that became too comfortable.

- As singles or couples, they continually fine tune their activity blends by talking things over with others who are attempting to achieve the same goal.

- They control the amount of time they spend in front of television.

- They made their movement into the Sweet Zone without giving up so much that they drifted too fast in the direction of the reflective zone.

- Most maintain good health programs (diet and exercise) so they are in shape to enjoy their outside activities.

A mid-course correction into the Sweet Zone can be a little like a midlife crisis. Slowing down can bring on periods of depression, giving up certain involvements can put the spotlight on the aging process, and attitude renewal is not always easy.

> Dr. Kelly made a smooth transition into his second life, things went extremely well for eight years. During this time he remained active (six hours in his office Monday, Wednesday, and Friday and four hours Saturday morning). This gave Dr. Kelly time for short fishing trips and vacations into various wilderness areas. He felt fulfilled, but started to worry about keeping up with medical advances. Finally his son, also an M.D., threatened to put a lock on his office door and throw the key away. "I decided at that point to give in. That was almost a year ago. How do I feel now? Great! I don't have to worry about malpractice suits anymore. I miss my patients less and less, I have more time with my wife and family, and I can enjoy a few social activities. Best of all, we can take more fishing trips and vacations. How sweet it is!"

BEHAVIORAL CHARACTERISTICS

What are some of the behavioral patterns of those who discover their own special Sweet Zones? Here are a few:

- Better planning for high-activity events and vacations.

- Earlier to bed, earlier to rise.

BEHAVIORAL CHARACTERISTICS
(Continued)

- Recovery days follow high activity days.

- More spontaneous laughter.

- Swings between high and low moods level out.

- Saying no to nonrewarding responsibilities becomes easier and more frequent.

- Disappointments handled with more tranquility.

- High activity events (fewer than in the past) are appreciated more.

- General behavior seems to indicate the individual is living in greater harmony with her or his own aging process.

In evaluating the "Sweet Zone" period, it should be remembered that some people can handle considerable social activity; others only need occasional people contact. Some individuals need a wide mix of outside and home activities; others like to specialize. Some people seem to take a few years to reach the balance necessary to find their own Sweet Zone; others, with good planning, seem to find it almost overnight.

SPECIAL REWARDS

What are some of the benefits to be found in the Sweet Zone—benefits not always available in other phases?

Living With Less Stress. You leave most stress behind when you enter your second life. Some stress is usually involved during the high-activity Serendipity Zone (part-time jobs, community activities, special goals). A Sweet Zone usually contains a minimum of stress.

No Need to Prove Yourself Again. Many people enter their second life with something to prove to others or to themselves. There is nothing wrong with this, but it is best for most people to accomplish their primary goals in zone two and seek greater inner fulfillment in zone three. Why keep fighting a battle when the war has been won?

Fewer Money Concerns. Most people enter their second life worried about the size of their money trees. Some use their precious time in zone two to grow a bigger tree. But by the time they reach the Sweet Zone they have come to terms with their income and available nest egg. Self-fulfillment becomes more important than money. A few cut loose and spend what they wish they had spent earlier.

ATTITUDES CAN MAKE THE SWEET ZONE SWEETER

What suggestions might you make to a loved one (parent, grandparent, friend) who is preparing to leave the Serendipity Zone?

- Waltzing can be as much fun as doing the samba.

- Quality in life is more important than quantity.

- Finding your own Sweet Zone may not mean you are getting older as much as it means you are getting smarter.

- Sweet Zone rewards may not bring as much outside recognition as inner pleasure.

- Live up to the motto "simplify to beautify" even if it means turning responsiblilities over to others.

- Continue to take trips, cruises, and vacations even if it means dipping into your capital.

What can be done to help people who stretch the Serendipity Zone beyond reason? How can they be convinced that the remaining zones offer pleasure/fulfillment opportunities? Everyone, of course, is free to accept or reject one or more zones. However, most people will be willing to make their midcourse correction under these conditions:

- When they see that stretching the Serendipity Zone has become counterproductive.

- When they desire a softer, quieter, more poetic comfort zone.

- When taking a nap improves the rest of the day.

- When they are endangering their health.

- When smelling the roses is more important than planting them.

Some obervers make the mistake of viewing the Sweet Zone as the "rocking chair" years old timers used to talk about. Not so! A sweet zone is that very special period in your second life that incorporates exciting activities of all kinds with some beautiful and comfortable home-oriented activities. The only period that might be viewed as a "rocking chair" period is the Spiritual Zone and even here, only to a limited extent. Those who ignore or misinterpret the rewards available with a Sweet Zone may miss the most valuable part of their second lives.

Chapter 4
ROCKING CHAIRS PERMITTED

> *"To me, old age is fifteen years older than I am."*
>
> Bernard Baruch

A time arrives when one can enjoy observing as much as participating—a reflective zone where some remaining pressures are put into the hands of others. The computer is on line, the course is set, but many new "thinking doors" have yet to be opened. Welcome to the Spiritual Zone!

Selecting a title for the fourth zone was most difficult. I finally took time to interview more people who had reached into their late eighties. I wanted to verify the caption or have them lead me to a better one. The Spiritual Zone won out over the runner up (Reflective Zone) for the following reasons.

- Many activities previously enjoyed are not as fulfilling as stretching the mind into new areas of contemplation.

- Mental growth (spiritual in nature or not) is the developmental part of this zone.

- During interviews, I was frequently offered a glass of wine, a fresh rose was often in the room, and a Bible was often nearby. This sent me a signal that the individual's mind was moving into new and exciting spiritual circles. Discussions reflected this change.

When I was talking about the Spiritual Zone and going on "automatic pilot" with my friend Sam who is 87, he replied: "I figure I have made the most of my life but I am hanging on by my teeth now. I know my body is on hold because it barely keeps going even when I stay with my simple routine. But my mind is not on automatic pilot. It's going full bore. That's the thing you've got to recognize at this stage. You may be forced to stay home much of the time to protect your body, but you can fly away mentally."

SLOWER BODY—MORE ACTIVE MIND

You reach the spiritual zone when it is difficult to maintain enough outside activity to balance home pleasures. Adding additional mind activities to go with simple home routine can be a source of satisfaction and, as one's world becomes smaller, other pleasures exist. Family and friends can come to visit. It is the perfect time to write one's memoirs. And television becomes a more enjoyable companion.

To someone aged 40, the Spiritual Zone may best be perceived as a zone where private time is valued. But this period should not be interpreted as "treading water." Rather, it is a rewarding arrangement between a *slow body and an active mind*. If some degree of bodily comfort can be maintained and the mind is challenged, the formula is right.

FLOATING INSTEAD OF SWIMMING

When people move out of their Sweet Zone into Spiritual, they discover they are happier floating than swimming. They find they can ignore big problems and laugh at the small ones. Consider the following.

Memory Time. Granted, people should do all they can to maintain their physical strength (housekeeping, walking, simple exercises), but it is their minds that carry them along. It is time to recall the beautiful (over and over if they wish) and forget mistakes.

Living With Less Fear. People in this zone seem to come to terms with their own mortality. Knowing their course is set helps them to push away fears. Often a sense of release leads to greater peace and tranquillity.

Attitude Magic. When some people reach the Spiritual Zone they view what is left in their lives with little enthusiasm. Others, at the same stage and with similar health problems, draw heavily on their memory to gear up their spirits. Result? They focus on the positive instead of the negative and discover that the magic of a positive attitude remains.

Television Becomes a Lifesaver. Those who have resisted excessive television during previous zones recognize that now is the time to indulge. Television becomes their window to the world. Instead of being an enemy to a more active and fulfilling life, it now becomes a blessing.

Spiritual Fulfillment. More than a few people have told me that they have found greater spiritual fulfillment in this zone than they had anticipated. Apparently after one has successfully lived through almost two lives, spiritual rewards are more accessible.

> Margaret is holding beautifully to her pleasures and fulfillments. Her primary pleasure is working in her garden. Despite her slow pace Margaret refuses even to consider hiring help. The daily compliments she receives from friends and strangers alike provide her with both identity and pride. Margaret attends church on a regular basis, has lunch at a senior center once each week, and accepts a few invitations to community events. She takes short trips to see a sister and other family members. Margaret comments: "Gus and I had a good life before he died. When I found myself alone, I started over. Traveled. Had some boy friends. Satisfied some dreams. Now I have a bagful of memories and a few day-to-day pleasures. Many do not value this time of life as I do. It's a shame, I've got what I appreciate most, and I'm still independent and free." Margaret is 84.

BEHAVIORAL CHARACTERISTICS

Whether living alone like Margaret or with others, rewarding patterns can often be maintained for several years. Living through previous zones gives one determination to extend this one. Some behavioral characteristics among those making the most out of the Spiritual Zone are:

- Laughing about forgetfulness or silly mistakes.

- Attempting to reminisce without repeating themselves or boring friends in other ways.

- Showing off a little.

- Looking years younger when they dress for an outside activity.

- Enjoying visitors.

- Trying to shock others through the use of untypical language, defending old-fashioned values, and spending money recklessly.

- Hearing what they want to hear even if they do not have a hearing impairment.

CONCLUSIONS

It is easy to conclude that those who reach the Spiritual Zone confine themselves to their living accommodations. Not so! All one need do to dispel this myth is to take a cruise. Although younger people aboard may participate in more activities, those in the Spiritual Zone miss out on very little. Many with canes, walkers, and wheelchairs keep remarkably active and add to the happy times of other passengers. Many are true Master Seniors* who demonstrate their class and style. One lady in her eighties who had received two hip replacements but continued to travel alone, summed up her attitude with this statement: ''I really should have spent more money earlier; but I have no regrets because now I can spend it taking these cruises, and that is exactly what I intend to do. I took the ''t'' out of can't years ago!''

My interviews have caused me to arrive at these conclusions:

- Those in the Spiritual Zone are more at ease with themselves.
- They are experts at conserving energy and judging their capacity to participate without overextending themselves.
- Many seem more content, perhaps because they have perfected the art of accepting those things they cannot change.
- Most are excellent conversationalists because they try harder to listen.
- Although their stories and jokes might not go over big on Saturday Night Live, they demonstrate concentration on the importance of a sense of humor.
- They fully appreciate the remaining rewards available to them.
- Their joys and fulfillments seem to run deeper.

---

*The idea of a Master Senior was first published in my book *Comfort Zones: A Practical Guide To Retirement Planning*. A Master Senior is an individual who has reached the age where it is recognized that she or he has *already* made a success of a second life.

HIGHER LEVELS OF FULFILLMENT

My general impression of those in the Spiritual Zone is that they have, through time, developed a special grace of involvement. They have learned they can reach a higher level of fulfillment by being more selective in their choices of activities. Is it because a slower tempo allows them to drink of life more deeply?

Although it was obvious that those I interviewed were putting their best foot forward, they demonstrated a strong sense of pride. This surfaced when we discussed living two lives instead of one and they recognized just how far they had come in their second life. These delighful and revealing conversations caused me to improve my own attitude in three ways. First, I lost some of the fear I had developed about becoming less active. Second, I received verification and reinforcement regarding the importance of a sense of humor (there was more laughter during these conversations than those with people in previous zones). Third, I discovered that not being able to sustain a high-level activity schedule does not prevent one from kicking up his or her heels on occasion.

These changes in my attitude made me feel more confident in writing about pleasure/fulfillment opportunities within the Spiritual Zone.

Chapter 5
SUNSET ZONE
THE UNFINISHED BUSINESS
OF LIVING

> *"It is impossible to experience one's death objectively—and still carry a tune."*
>
> Woody Allen

It was easy to settle on the title for this zone because on three different interviews I heard variations of the phrase: "You know, I am looking into the sunset." These comments were not made with an overtone of regret over the past or fear of the future. People near 90 or over are thankful for their full lives and seem to have only modest apprehension about entering their own safe harbors. Their primary anxiety is to make sure they have time to wind up the unfinished business of their lives.

Unfinished business includes adjustments to wills and trusts, a final letter of instruction regarding the disposition of personal effects, and, in some cases, reconciliations. At this stage, help from family members or professionals is frequently required. The good news is that spiritual growth can continue.

REACHING A SAFE HARBOR

Do you remember the sense of relief you experienced upon arriving home after a long, dangerous, and frustrating trip? If so, you may agree that reaching a safe harbor (death) can turn out to be a positive, spiritual experience. In field-testing the *Second Life Planning Guide* (see page 75), I sought replies to the question:

> *Do you believe that by accepting the Sunset Zone ahead of time that earlier zones are enhanced?*

Seven out of 10 individuals answered "yes." In follow-up conversations, I was able to ask why they gave positive answers. Three typical replies follow.

> "I think it is easier to accept death if you know you have lived two successful lives instead of one."

> "My guess is that making the most of earlier stages gives life more meaning and death becomes more of a triumph."

> "Until you accept the Sunset Zone you are riddled with fears that destroy the earlier zones."

It is intriguing to note that different people in different zones told me one reason they wanted to reach the Sunset Zone was to "see as much history unfold as possible." This frequent comment tells me that those who maintain a positive curiosity about the changes in modern society make the most out of their later years.

An interesting parallel can be made between what takes place in retirement planning and what happens in winding up the details of one's second life. When individuals get ready to leave their careers, they check out their Social Security provisions, private pensions, insurance programs, and attend a few farewell events. When people prepare to leave their second lives, they want to complete funeral arrangements and many other details. Both procedures can be viewed as *unfinished business*.

BECOMING COMFORTABLE WITH YOUR OWN MORTALITY

Everyone I interviewed said they would prefer a short Sunset Zone so morbidity is compressed and where institutional confinement is avoided. But, regardless of the circumstances (destiny) life hands them, most had become comfortable with the future and had discovered a spiritual grace that would see them through.

Beverly Sanborn, a researcher into aging in Southern California, was quoted in the *Los Angeles Times* as being fascinated because, as a whole, the old-old are not afraid of death as many assume.'' She states: ''Our culture is petrified at the thought of death. But not these people. They talk openly and often about it. They seem to have a real sense of moving on to something else. Maybe they are closer to a life truth.''

Among those I interviewed, it would appear that the most widely accepted poem appropriate for the Sunset Zone is by Alfred, Lord Tennyson.

CROSSING THE BAR

Sunset and evening star,
And one clear call for me
And may there be no moaning of the bar
When I put out to sea.

But such a tide as moving seems asleep,
Too full for sound or foam.
When that which drew from out the boundless deep
Turns again home.

Twilight and evening bell,
And after that the dark.
And may there be no sadness of farewell
When I embark.

For tho from out our bourne of Time and place
The food may bear me far.
I hope to see my pilot face to face.
When I have crossed the bar.
